The Son
of a
Sharecropper

The Son *of a* Sharecropper

A Time to Remember

A Memoir by
Billy Spencer

Columbus, Ohio

The Son Of A Sharecropper: A Time to Remember

Published by Gatekeeper Press
2167 Stringtown Rd, Suite 109
Columbus, OH 43123-2989
www.GatekeeperPress.com

Copyright © 2018 by Billy Spencer
All rights reserved. Neither this book, nor any parts within it may be sold or reproduced in any form or by any electronic or mechanical means, including information storage and retrieval systems without permission in writing from the author. The only exception is by a reviewer, who may quote short excerpts in a review.

ISBN (paperback): 9781642373998

Library of Congress Number: 2018964883

Printed in the United States of America

Books by Billy Spencer

THE SON OF A SHARECROPPER
JEZEBEL, QUEEN OF EVIL
RUTH, PORTRAIT OF GRACE
ONESIMUS, THE FORGIVEN FUGITIVE
CROWNED IN CRISIS
THE THRILLING ADVENTURES OF KING DAVID

Booklets

REACH HIGHER
THE GREATEST SECRET

Dedication

This book is dedicated to Grandma Minnie, my parents, Charlie and Rhoda Spencer, who are now in heaven.

Also, to my wife, Shirley, my children, Mark and Cindy, my brother, Edward, my dear friend Ruby Williams, Valta Ree Casselman, my cousins, and to the generations of relatives yet to come, who may be interested in how the son of a sharecropper survived in the cotton patch during the Great Depression.

Contents

PART ONE: 13
The Great Adventure
Two Mules And A Plow

PART TWO: 57
The Cotton Patch
A Time To Remember

PART THREE: 133
The Way We Were
Through It All

Acknowledgements

It would be monumental arrogance for me to fail to give thanks to those who assisted me in the research and writing of this book.

I thank my wife, Shirley, who conceived the idea, and for many hours of transcription and editorial work.

I want to thank my son, Mark, and daughter, Cindy, for their encouragement and insistence that this book be written.

I also wish to express my profound gratitude to Ruby Williams, for information and pictures, and for her deep interest and constant encouragement.

I thank my cousin, Dean Davis Lee, for her insight into the thirteen months she and her family lived with us in the Deep Fork River Bottom.

My thanks to Kathy Crosby for providing historical pictures from the Henryetta Library.

I thank Valta Ree Darnell Casselman for her thoughts while teaching at Bartlett School.

I also express my gratitude to the staff at Gatekeeper Press, for their guidance and incredible patience with me.

Also, my thanks to John Grisham, whose writings have brought to my remembrance stories that are strikingly similar to my experiences as a young boy in the cotton patch, although, in a different time and place, and with different characters.

And last of all, to my brother, Edward, and wife Marion, who provided pictures, dates, places, people, and stories that I had forgotten.

I am so grateful to have lived during that period of history which I write about, but I'm also grateful that I have no more cotton to pick. I have been blessed beyond measure.

Part One

The Great Adventure

Two Mules And A Plow

Chapter 1

My name is Billy Spencer. I am the son of a sharecropper, and this is my story. It is a true story, a story that began when I was born in the rural community of Fair Grove, Missouri, on August 25, 1932.

My father, Charlie, and my mother, Rhoda, were from Oklahoma. They were married when he was nineteen and she was fifteen. My brother Edward was born in Muskogee, Oklahoma, August 4, 1930.

My story will take you from Missouri, to the cotton fields of western Oklahoma during the Great Depression, to the Promise Land of California in 1934, then, back again to Oklahoma in the winter of 1939 where we made our home in the deep fork river bottom, which is located about seven miles east of Henryetta, between Deep Fork River and Tiger Mountain.

It was my experiences in the cotton patch that shaped and molded this insignificant, unworthy, farm boy into the person I am today.

My brother Ed and I were too young to remember the first part of our journey, but our parents filled in that part before they died. The rest of the story is my recollection with the help of my older brother Ed, and a few others still living.

So let's begin at the beginning. My parents were living in Muskogee, Oklahoma, in 1930, the year my brother was born. By the spring of 1932, they had moved just outside the rural community of Fair Grove, Missouri, where my father was fortunate to find work on a dairy farm. His job, among other things, was to milk 37 cows by hand, twice a day. He was paid one dollar a day, a place to live, and all the milk our family could drink. I was born in late August of that same year.

In late August of 1933, my mother's sister, Bessie, and her husband, Perry Stewart, came to visit us. My mother had five brothers and three sisters, of which she was the youngest.

"Charlie," Perry said. "Go with us to western Oklahoma. I hear they need cotton pickers around the Gotebo area. At seventy-five cents a hundred pounds, you can make three or four times the money you're making here."

My father was reluctant about leaving the security of his job. The country was in a deep depression, and jobs were hard to come by.

"Charlie," my mother said. "I think we should go."

My parents had come to Missouri by bus and had no means of transportation. With two babies to care for, my mother was depressed and felt trapped with no hope of a future. She was willing to gamble on a new adventure.

Finally, my father relented and agreed to go. They informed the owner of the dairy, packed what few things they had in Perry's car, and with their two babies, left Missouri and headed west on Route 66.

When they reached Weatherford, Oklahoma, they turned south on a dirt road. Soon there were fields of cotton on both sides of the road. Just outside of Gotebo, Perry turned up a lane that led to a farm house.

"Are you hiring cotton pickers?" Perry asked the owner of the farm.

"Oh yes," he said. "All the pickers I can get. The cotton is ready to pick. I pay seventy-five cents a hundred."

"There are four of us, and some babies," Perry said. "Do you know where we might camp out?"

The owner pointed to a one room shack on the north end of the cotton field. "You're welcome to camp there."

How my mother managed to look after two babies and pick cotton is beyond me. My father picked an average of five-hundred pounds of cotton a day. It was hard work, but they were making more money than they ever had before.

By the end of October the cotton had been picked. One evening, just before dark, my parents walked to the farm house to thank the owner for the opportunity of a job. The owner and his wife invited them to stay for supper. While they were gone, Perry and Bessie loaded up their belongings and left without telling my parents. They were left stranded with no means of transportation.

The owner of the farm had an old Model-T-Ford parked behind his barn. It did not run. My father purchased the car for thirty-five dollars, and for the next several weeks he worked on the old car and finally got it running. He bought two used spare tires, two cans of tube patching, and two five gallon cans for gasoline, and some bailing wire.

In January of 1934, my parents packed what little they had into the car, and with my brother and I bundled up, left the cotton fields and headed north. When we hit Route 66 we turned west, along with many other people migrating west during the Great Depression. My father had been told that jobs were to be had in California.

They learned later that Perry and Bessie had settled in San Bernardino. Another sister, Elsie, and her husband, Richard, were already settled in Palm City. Several days later, we arrived in California at a place called Crows Landing near Modesto. We were there only a short time. We then traveled to Palm City and stayed with my mother's sister, Elsie, for a few days, before renting a house near them.

My father was fortunate to land a job as grounds keeper at the Del Coronado Golf Course. His salary was 100 dollars a month. After the first year, his salary increased to 130 dollars per month. In time, he managed to purchase two lots within a couple of blocks of my uncle and aunts house. My uncle helped my father build a small box house on the property.

When we were old enough, my brother Ed and I enrolled in school. This was when I began to remember things. My father traded the old Model-T- for a 1929 Model-A-Ford. Model A's have a peculiar sound when the engine is running. When my father would come home from work, Ed and I would listen for that peculiar sound. You could hear it coming two or three blocks away from the house. We would run up the street to meet our father. He would slow down and let us jump on the running board and ride to the house.

Occasionally on Sunday's, my mother would pack a lunch and we would head for the beach where our father taught us how to swim. We were a happy family, living the great American dream.

THE SON OF A SHARECROPPER

1935
Charlie Spencer age 26, Edward age 5,
Billy age 3, Rhoda Spencer age 22

Edward and Billy Spencer in California

Edward and Billy, Palm City, California

In August of 1939, my brother and I had birthdays. He was nine years old, and I was seven. That fall a motion picture was coming to a theater in Chula Vista that we wanted to see. It was called, "Tarzan Finds A Son." We were so excited. We had never seen a movie before. When it arrived at the theater, we loaded into our Model-A-Ford and left for Chula Vista.

We had seen about half the movie when a policeman and an usher moved quickly down the theater aisle, his flashlight shinning, yelling, "Is there a Mr. Spencer here?"

My father stood, saying, "I'm Spencer, what is it?"

"Your house is on fire!" the policeman said.

We rushed out of the theater to our car. The policeman said he would escort us to our home in Palm City. As we neared Palm City, we saw an orange glow in the sky.

"That's our house," my father said.

My mother began to cry. I looked at my brother and his eyes were big as saucers. We were scared to death.

We only saw the first half of the movie, and it left me wondering if Tarzan was ever able to escape that alligator. But because of the crisis we now faced, our excitement of seeing a movie was crushed, and the life we were living was now in jeopardy.

As we came near where our house used to be, there was a crowd of people milling around. When the car stopped, we all jumped out. My parents wanted to see if there was anything left to salvage. There was nothing left but smoke and ashes.

All that we had were the clothes on our back. We were fortunate to be able to stay with my mother's sister until my parents could decide on what they should do. The next day we went to the Salvation Army. They gave us boxes of canned food and several changes of clothes. There will always be a place in my heart for the Salvation Army.

Sometime later, I overheard my parents talking about going back to Oklahoma. My mother had another sister living in Henryetta, Oklahoma. "We could stay with my sister Cordie, until we settled somewhere," she told my father.

A few weeks later, we packed our things in our 1929 Model-A-Ford and headed to Oklahoma. My father was hoping to find a place to farm. We had lived in California for five years, and the person I missed most was my second grade teacher, Miss Haden. I think I had a crush on her.

We arrived in Henryetta a few days later. Uncle George and Aunt Cordie insisted that we stay with them while we looked for a place of our own. We lived with them for three weeks. Aunt Cordie was very nice to us. Uncle George, a full blood Creek Indian, stayed at the Pool Hall most of the time.

After Christmas, my father arranged a sharecropping agreement with a man named Mr. Swan. The land was about seven miles east of Henryetta. There was around 40 to 60 acres east of Coal Creek that could be farmed, and about 30 acres west of the creek. Mr. Swan said we could move into a two room house that was on the property. There was also a four room house a quarter of a mile around the bend of the creek that might be available later. Whatever we raised, the owner would get half the profits. The rest, after expenses, would be ours. My father seemed excited about it, but my mother was not so sure.

We drove east from Henryetta on highway 266 through the small town of Dewar. Continuing east, just before crossing the Deep Fork River bridge, we turned south on a dirt road. After about half a mile, we came to a small community called Bartlett. As we started down a hill, I noticed a schoolhouse on the right, a house on the left, and only three houses on the west side of the road. At the bottom of the hill was a grocery store.

I would later learn about the people who lived in those houses. The house across from the school is where the Wilson's lived. They owned the store at the bottom of the hill. Their kids were Max, Irvin, Leroy, and Myrna. They were older than my brother and I. Opposite the Wilson's was Herma Carr and her mother's house. As we drove down the hill, there were no houses on the east side of the road, but on the west was a house for teachers, then the Williams place. Floyd and Gladys had two boys, Richard and Roy, also Gladys' mother, Ella Wallace, lived with them. Richard would become one of my best friends over the next few years.

Just beyond the Grocery Store was a Depot on the north side of the railroad tracks which ran east and west. A Motor Coach would stop to pick up passengers going to Henryetta, or back toward Muskogee, making stops along the way.

We drove up and over the tracks and turned east on the road to the river bottom. We had to cross a rickety board plank bridge over a slough. After another quarter of a mile, we turned south and finally came to an old two room shack that we were to live in. It was in terrible shape. We would spend the next few weeks living there.

An old two-room shack much like our
first house in the river bottom

My mother opened the door of the house and stood staring in silence. The floors were rotted and warped. You could see daylight between the clap boards of the house. Rats scampered across the floor and disappeared down a hole. She shook her head in disgust and said to my father, "Charlie, this is awful."

"Well," he answered. "We'll just camp out here a while and take a look at the other house, maybe Mr. Swan will let us move there."

"I don't see how we can spend the winter here," my mother told him.

My father busied himself clearing a place where he could build a fire. After all it was winter. My mother swept the floor of the house and laid down some quilts for us to sleep on. I slept very little that first night. You could hear the rats running across the floor.

The next morning my mother cooked oats over an outside fire. She was not a happy person.

On Saturday we drove out of the river bottom and stopped at Wilson's store. Gladys Williams was coming out of the store as we were going in. She stopped and introduced herself. She already knew we had moved to the river bottom. We would soon learn that news travels quickly in this small community.

"I need to get my kids enrolled in school," my mother stated.

"The school has been on a break for the holidays, but it starts again on Monday. I have two boys about the age of yours. Grace Rose is their teacher. The number of students varies from year to year, but this year there will be about twenty from grades one through eight," Gladys said proudly.

"Thank you Gladys. I look forward to getting better acquainted with you. We are on our way to Henryetta. Charlie is hoping to find some used farming equipment, and of course, I need some things as well."

From the store to the top of the hill was perhaps a quarter of a mile. As we passed the grade school, I glanced at the basketball goal at the end of a dirt court and dreamed that someday I would be a star basketball player.

Another half mile down the dusty road, we turned west on highway 266. The distance from our farm to Henryetta was approximately seven miles. At thirty miles an hour, the trip took about twenty minutes or so. As we came into Henryetta, we passed a gas station. They advertised gas for 12 cents a gallon, and kerosene at 10 cents a gallon.

There were a lot of people in town. My father heard that there would be a farm auction that afternoon at the Farmer's Cotton Gin, which was located west of Main Street near the railroad track.

Near the Cotton Gin was an open area of used farm equipment, mules, horses, pigs, and chickens. People were already milling around, inspecting items of interest to them.

"We'll go up town and you boys can go to a movie. I'll come back for the auction," my father told us.

There were two movie theaters in town, the Blaine and Morgan. My mother gave us 15 cents each, ten cents for the movie, and five cents for a soda pop. The Morgan Theater was showing a movie starring Gene Autry, so we decided to go there. We were very excited.

"When the movie is over, stay here in front of the theater and I will come and get you," mother said. "I will do some shopping while you are at the movie."

While we were at the movie, my mother bought us two Big Chief writing tablets and two pencils for school. I learned on the way home that my father was able to win the bid on a pair of mules with harnesses, a two row walking cultivator, a turning plow, and wagon. He made arrangements for a man to deliver them to our farm. He also purchased cotton and corn seed, as well as some vegetable seed.

Two days later the mules and farm equipment were delivered to us. My father had them unload everything at the old barn where the four-room house was located. We were now in the farming business.

BILLY SPENCER

Fall of 1940
Charlie Spencer, our mules, Pete and
Kate, and uncle Earl Cooley

Chapter 2

Mrs. Rose was a stern teacher. She would spend a half hour with each grade. There were eight grades, and she had from one to five students in each grade. The best part of school for me was recess. I would get to play basketball with my school friends, including some girls, like Helen Berry, and Charlene Walling.

It was a cold winter, and my brother Ed and I walked to school each day. The lunch our mother prepared for us would be two biscuits with rabbit meat. They were so good. On occasion, she would give us a nickel to buy a soda pop. I was always tempted to get a big Royal Crown Cola because it was a big bottle, but after tasting a Grapette, even though it was much smaller, I would get it.

A couple of weeks after we were in school there was a big snow storm. My father tied burlap sacks around our feet, and Ed and I walked out of the river bottom in several inches of snow. The snow came up past my knees in places. We were frozen by the time we got to school. The school had a pot-bellied stove to warm us up. Thank God for that.

It was March of 1940 when my father received permission to relocate to the four room house, which was a quarter of a mile around the bend of the creek. It was a house the Gulf Oil Company built for workers to use when drilling for oil back in the 1920's. It had a front and back porch, a kitchen, living room, and two bedrooms. There was no electricity, water, or inside bathroom. It had a cistern for catching water off the roof of the house when it rained, a well house, a smoke house, an outhouse, and an old dilapidated barn. There was a pecan tree in front of the house, and a Cottonwood tree between the house and the oil field tool shed.

There was gas piped in from a gas well to the kitchen, so my father bought a used gas stove for my mother. She was elated. She finally had a place she could call home. However, the next year the oil company shut down the gas well, so my father bought my mother a used kerosene cook stove. We also used kerosene lamps for lighting.

Spring was around the corner. My father hitched up the two mules and began breaking ground. He named the two mules Pet and Kate. He planted 40 acres of cotton and 30 acres of corn.

We also purchased a milk cow, chickens, and two sows that had two litters of pigs. My mother managed to have a very large garden which provided us with vegetables. We learned to live off the land with all kinds of wild game to eat.

Other than the Conklin family who lived a quarter of a mile or so up the creek, we were fairly isolated.

By May, my father had finished planting the corn and cotton. It was time to do some hunting. He taught my brother and I how to shoot his Remington 22 rifle. With plenty of rabbits, squirrels, and a big garden, we had plenty to eat.

Boots Conklin had two brothers, Luke and Fred, who lived with their widowed mother. Boots was three years older than I was, but we became best buddies. We would hunt together a lot.

One day as we were coming back from the river, walking along the railroad tracks, we spotted a crow way up in the top of a tall pecan tree some hundred and fifty feet away.

"Here," Boots said. "Rest your rifle on my shoulder to steady it, and take a shot at that crow."

I aimed and took a shot. The crow toppled from its perch and fell to the ground.

"You sure shoot good for a seven year old, Billy," she said.

"I know it," I answered, so proud of myself.

My brother and I went barefoot from spring until late fall. We could walk anywhere we wanted because of the thick leathery tissue we had developed on the bottom of our feet.

Before long, it was time for us to try and find people to help us chop cotton and corn. We needed to thin the cotton and corn to about twelve inches apart, and chop the weeds out. The weeds grew fast in the middle of summer, so as soon as we finished chopping once, it was time to chop again. So we needed help.

Although my grandmother and her husband Amon would help us, we needed more choppers. I have heard my mother say that Amon was Grandma Minnie's seventh husband, but I had my doubts. Exaggeration was a Spencer trait.

I couldn't understand why anybody would want to spend ten hours a day in the hot sweltering sun for most of the summer chopping cotton, but that's what we did.

One Saturday while eating lunch, my father said he would be going to town to look for some field hands to help us chop our cotton. "You boys want to go with me," my father asked.

Ed wanted to go rabbit hunting, so I went with my father. I sat in the front seat with my father as he drove our 1929 Model-A-Ford out of the river bottom. We went up and over the railroad tracks and parked in front of Wilson's store. We got out of the car, and I waited outside the store until my father nodded in the direction of the store. That was my cue to go in and purchase a soda pop, on credit. It cost a nickel, but it was not a foregone conclusion he would nod. While he was talking to Mr. Wilson, I would go in the store anyway and loiter around long enough for Mrs. Wilson to sneak me a piece of hard candy, which always came with strict instructions not to tell my father. Charlie Spencer was a poor man, but he was intensely proud. He would have whipped me if he knew I had accepted a piece of candy, so Mrs. Wilson had no trouble swearing me to secrecy.

But this time I got the nod. As always, Mrs. Wilson was dusting the counter when I entered and gave me a stiff hug. I was torn between a Grapette soda and a Baby Ruth candy bar. Since they were both a nickel, I chose the candy bar this time. I signed the charge slip with great flair, and she inspected my penmanship.

"It's getting better, Billy," she said.

"Not bad for a seven year old," I said.

"Where's your father?"

It was Mrs. Wilson's calling in life to monitor the movements of the community's population, so any question was usually answered with another.

"He's outside," I answered. "We're goin' to town to look for people to help us chop cotton."

"Not many people want to do that kind of work, but maybe you'll find some," she said. "Are you going to be a farmer?"

"No ma'am, a basketball player." I bit into my candy bar and chewed it slowly while rewrapping and pocketing the other half.

My father opened the door just wide enough to stick his head in. "Let's go," he said; then, "Howdy Mrs. Wilson."

"Howdy Charlie," she said as she patted my head and sent me away.

When we came to the highway, we turned west toward Henryetta. I watched my father carefully shift gears—pressing slowly on the clutch, delicately prodding the gear shift until the car reached the perfect speed of thirty miles per hour. His theory was that every automobile had a speed at which it ran most efficiently, and through some vaguely defined method he had determined that his old car should go thirty. My mother said (to me) that it was ridiculous. She suspected he drove much faster when he was alone.

When the car reached the cruising speed, I looked over to check the speedometer; thirty. He smiled at me as if we both agreed that the car belonged at that speed. There was very little traffic on the highway, but on the rare occasion a car passed us, my father's favorite sayings was, "Go on, we'll walk." It was approximately seven miles to town, but coming out of the river bottom, and slowing down through the small town of Dewar, the trip took around twenty minutes. It took as long to get out of the river bottom and reach the highway, as it did to get from the highway to Henryetta.

We drove up Main Street and turned north at the railroad tracks. The owner of the Farmers Cotton Gin allowed part of his property to be a staging area for migrant workers. They could be hired by farmers to chop cotton in the summer and pick it in the fall.

We parked and waited. I glanced over at my father's handsome face, then his hands resting on the steering wheel. They were calloused from working on the farm. My mother told me that when he was eighteen he joined the Circus as a boxer. At each town he would take on all comers. Those who challenged him would put up two dollars with the promise of winning five dollars if they beat him. No one ever did. Charlie Spencer, my father, was only five-feet-seven, but he was all man. I saw him lift a five-hundred pound section of a discarded iron rail from the railroad tracks, balance it on his shoulder and cross the creek on a foot log, then upend it on the other side. It was used to break up the clods after the ground was plowed. My father could do anything. I loved my daddy.

In my father's opinion, it was the best spot in the county to catch field workers. I wasn't so sure. I pulled out the rest of my candy bar and offered my father a bite. "No son, you eat it."

We got out of the car and sat on the running board in complete silence for half an hour. No one showed up. We walked across the field to the home of the owner of the cotton gin to let him know we needed cotton choppers, and if any stopped to inquire about work, please send them to the deep fork river bottom. He said he would. We got back in the car and headed home.

We stopped again at Wilson's store to see if we had any mail. I waited for a nod from my father. It never came. There was a letter from Grandma Minnie, and a letter from Palm City, California, which he opened and was silent for a moment.

"It's a letter from a lawyer," he told me. "The lawyer wants to buy our two lots we own in California."

"You gonna sell them?" I asked.

"The lawyer said he would give us two hundred dollars for them. What do you think I should do?"

"Wow, daddy, that's a lot of money."

"We'll see what your mother has to say about it," he said, as he opened the letter from my grandmother. She lived in Muskogee.

"It looks like your grandmother and Amon will be here on Monday, Billy boy."

The letter said she and Amon would arrive on the Motor Coach (Gladys Williams called it Coal-oil-Johnny). The small shack of a depot was across from Wilson's store. We would pick them up there.

I was glad my grandmother was coming. They would help us chop cotton, and that meant less cotton for me to chop.

My grandmother was four feet eight inches tall with long hair she kept tied in a bundle on the back of her head.

She was born in 1880 in Indian Territory. She was one half Cherokee Indian.

When my father told my mother that his mother and Amon would be arriving on Monday, I could tell she was not very happy about their coming. It would mean sharing the kitchen with Minnie and would be taking the bedroom

Motor Car, or Dinky and Dootlebug as some called it. Gladys Williams called it "Coal Oil Johnny"

where Ed and I slept. We would sleep on a pallet on the floor of our living room. But she knew it was a necessary inconvenience. We needed choppers.

Dad sold the two lots in California for two hundred dollars, which would allow him to hire more field hands if he could find them.

My mother had a passion for cleanliness. My brother and I got a complete scrubbing every Saturday afternoon whether we needed it or not. We would draw water from the well and fill a washtub half full, and sit in it while mamma scrubbed our neck and ears. She would leave the private parts to us. When we stepped out of the tub, the water would be muddy.

THE SON OF A SHARECROPPER

Dad left on Monday to pick up Grandma and Amon at the depot. When they arrived back at our house, Grandma stepped out of the car, stretched out her arms and said, "There's my boys." She hugged us and we went into the house where momma had prepared lunch for us all. It was fried rabbit, potatoes and gravy, tomatoes, onions, cucumbers, and biscuits. I cleaned my plate as I was always instructed to do, and was full as a tick, as Grandma would say.

Amon and Grandma Minnie

1929 Model-A-Ford and the Spencer boys,
Ed and Billy in summer of 1940

The Deep Fork River Bottom

Chapter 3

The Great Depression came early and stayed late in rural Oklahoma. The only farmers who made money were those who owned their own land. Most sharecroppers were doomed to eternal poverty.

But my father's goal was to own forty acres of land, free and clear. My mother's dreams were tucked away, only to be shared with her boys as we grew older. But I already knew she longed to leave the rural life, and was determined that her boys would not farm. By the end of the first year of chopping and picking cotton, she had made a believer out of me.

We chopped cotton for most of the summer of 1940. One day while taking a break for my father to sharpen our hoes, our hounds began barking. There was a family of black folks walking toward us.

"I wonder what they want," my father mused.

I counted seven people. They carried burlap sacks over their shoulders. I assumed it was their belongings.

"My name is Jim Nolan, and this is my family. Mr. Wilson told us you may be hiring farm hands."

"Well, I'm Charlie, and yes, we could use some help. Where are you from?"

"Grayson. We been walkin' most of the mornin' lookin' for work. When we got to Wilson's store, that's when we heard you might be hirin'."

The couple had five children. There were three girls much older than I was, and two boys who looked to be about the same age as Ed and I.

"You must be thirsty, hungry I bet," my father stated.

"Yas'um."

"Let's walk back to the house. You can sit on the porch and we'll get you some water," my father said.

"We sho thank yah Mr. Challee."

My mother went ahead of us to fix a plate of food for them.

Jim and Mammy Nolan sat in chairs on the porch, the kids sat on the edge of the porch. The Nolan's were quite lucky, because my mother believed that no one living within walking distance of our farm would ever go without food.

Mr. Nolan said, as he wiped his mouth with the back of his hand, "We is hard workin', God fearin' folks Challee."

"I pay one dollar and fifty cents a day, and we work ten hours a day. Do you have a place to stay?" my father asked.

"No suh."

"There's a two room shack back around the creek. We stayed there part of last winter. It's not much, but you're welcome to camp out there."

"You is a good man, Challee. We'll clean it up and make do. Thank yah."

I looked at the girls sitting on the edge of the porch. I knew they were younger than my mother, but certainly a lot older than I was. The oldest girl looked to be maybe seventeen, and the youngest girl perhaps thirteen. But it was the one in between those two, with big brown eyes and hair pulled tightly behind her head that drew my attention. I looked at her in her tattered dress and long legs. She was pretty, I thought. She looked at me and smiled.

"What's your name," she asked.

"Billy," I said, kicking a rock. My cheeks were immediately warm. "What's yours?"

"Jessie. How old are you?"

"Seven. How old are you?"

"Fifteen."

"You walk all the way from Grayson?"

"Sure did. Been walkin' all mornin'."

She was barefoot and her dress was soiled, but I thought she was perfect. This was the first time I remembered really examining a girl. She watched me with a knowing smile, and then gazed thoughtfully across the cotton field. I think she likes me.

I pointed to the boy I thought was near my age. "What's your name?"

"Wilber."

"Nice to meet you Wilbur. How old are you?"

"Eight. My brother over there is nine. His name is Sonny."

Sonny must have had hand me down breeches, because they were short. They came halfway between his knees and ankles. Grandma would say he had on high water breeches. She had lots of sayings.

"You ever play basketball?"

"Nope."

"I don't have a basketball, but I have a toe sack rolled up and tied. When we're not workin' in the cotton, maybe you and Sonny can come over and shoot some baskets with us. I have a basketball goal on the well house."

"If ma and pa will let us, I'd like to play with ya'll."

"Meet us here at six in the morning," my father told Mr. Nolan. " We break for lunch and quit at five. I have hoes for all of you and a jug of water."

When they were gone, my mother suggested that we pick a bushel of vegetables and take it to them. I volunteered to take it.

I had never seen a black person before. To me they were just people with dark skin, and not much darker than me. I was part Cherokee Indian and had a deep sun tan.

"Do you like them?" I asked my father.

"They are good people son, they are just different."

"I guess we're just lucky to have them, ain't we?"

"Yes we are."

More field hands meant less choppin' for me and my brother. For the next several weeks we would go to the field at sunrise. The hoes would be sharpened the night before. I would pick a row as near as I could get to Jessie, and stare for a moment at the endless row of cotton, afraid to look down the row and be reminded of how endless it was. By the end of the day my arms would ache, and my back would hurt. Yes, I wanted all the help in the field I could get, especially if they were as nice as Jessie.

Wolf Creek was located south of us near Tiger Mountain. The water was clear and a good place to swim near the low water dam. Ed and I went there often during the summer. And then there was Shorty's Pond, a deep hole of water a mile or so from the house near the river. Max Wilson and his brothers would come to our place on some Sunday's and ask my mother if Ed and I could go swimming with them. Max, who was eighteen, convinced my mother that he would look after her boys.

We were told to never swim in the river, but we did. The muddy water of the river irritated our eyes, and mamma could always tell that we had disobeyed her, and we knew that a whippin' was coming. We had no bathing suit, we swam in our birthday suits. It was called "Skinny Dipping."

Going without a shirt all summer, I developed a dark tan. I suppose being part Indian helped. In fact, Jessie wasn't much darker that I was.

One Sunday afternoon, when most of the family was doing small chores, or trying to nap, Jessie came by the house. I was shooting hoops with my rolled up burlap sack. She was carrying a small bag. She was barefoot and wearing the same tight dress she'd been wearing the first time I'd seen her.

"Hi Billy. Will you do me a favor?" she asked ever so sweetly.

My cheeks turned red. I had no idea what favor she wanted, but there was no doubt she'd get it from me. "What?" I asked, trying to be difficult.

"The creek by our house looks so nasty, is there some other place I could go to take a bath?"

"Well, the best place would be Wolf Creek. It's about a half mile that way (I pointed) this side of Tiger Mountain."

"Is the water clear, not muddy?"

"Should be clear, it hasn't rained for a while."

She looked around to make sure no one was listening, then said, "Will you go with me?"

My heart stopped, and my mouth was suddenly dry. "Why?" I managed to ask.

She grinned again and rolled her eyes away.

"I don't know," she cooed. "To make sure nobody sees me."

She could've said, "Because I don't know where the creek is," or "to make sure there was no snakes." Or something, anything that had nothing to do with seeing her bathe.

But she didn't.

"Are you scared?" I asked.

"Maybe a little."

We cut across the field until the house and barn was out of sight, then followed a path to the creek. Trees lined both sides of the creek, so in the summer it was usually a cool place to swim.

I led her down to the low water dam where the water was deepest. "This is a good spot," I said.

The water was clear. "The water comes up to about here," I said, touching a spot on my chest.

"There's nobody around is there?" She seemed a little nervous.

"No, everybody is back at the farm."

"You go back up the trail and look out for me, okay?"

"Okay," I said without moving.

"Go on, Billy," she said, placing her bag on the bank.

"Okay," I said, and started back up the trail.

"And, Billy, no peeking, okay?"

I felt like I'd just been caught. I waved her off as if the thought had never crossed my mind. "Of course not," I said.

I crawled up the bank and found a spot a few feet above the ground, on the limb of an elm tree, high enough to see if someone was approaching.

"Billy!" she called.

"Yes!"

"Is everything clear?"

"Yep!"

I heard water splash but kept my eyes to the north. After a minute or two, I slowly turned around and looked down the creek. I couldn't see her, and was somewhat relieved.

Another minute passed, and I began to feel useless. No one knew we were here, so no one would be trying to sneak up on her. How often would I have the chance to see a pretty girl bathing? I wondered what Ed would do if he were here. I could recall no specific reason, though I knew it was wrong. But maybe it wasn't terribly sinful.

I climbed down from the elm limb and sneaked through the weeds and brush until I was near the creek.

Her dress and underclothes were hung over a bush. Jessie was waist deep in the water, her head was covered with white lather as she gently washed her hair. I was sweating, but not breathing. Lying on my stomach in the grass, peering through the weeds, I was invisible to her.

She dipped her head under the water, rinsing out the soap, sending the lather away in the slight current. Then she stood, her back to me, and I saw her rear end, all of it. She was wearing nothing, which is what I wore when I went swimming, and it was what I expected. But confirming it sent a shudder through my body. Instinctively, I raised my head, I guess for a better look, then ducked again when I regained my senses.

If she caught me, she'd tell her father, who'd tell my father, who'd beat me until I couldn't walk. I'd be ruined.

In the water up to her waist, she bathed her arms and chest, which I could see from the side. I had never seen a woman's breast before, and I doubt if any seven year old boy in Bartlett had. I was certain no boy my age had ever had this view.

A wicked thought came from nowhere. Having seen most of her privates, I now wanted to see everything. If I yelled "snake!" at the top of my voice, she would scream in horror. She would forget the soap and wash cloth, her nudity and all that, and she would scamper for dry land. She would go for her clothes, but for a few glorious seconds I would see it all.

I swallowed hard, tried to clear my throat, but realized how dry my mouth was. With my heart racing away, I hesitated, and in doing so learned a valuable lesson in patience.

To wash her legs, Jessie stepped closer to the bank. She rose from the water until the water covered nothing but her feet. Slowly, with the soap and wash cloth she bent and stretched and caressed her long legs and buttocks and stomach. My heart pounded.

She rinsed by splashing water over her body. And when she was finished, and still standing in ankle-deep water, wonderfully naked, Jessie turned and stared directly at the spot where I happened to be hiding.

I dropped my head and burrowed even deeper into the weeds. I waited for her to yell something, but she did not. This sin was unforgiveable, I was now certain.

I inched backward, very slowly, not making a sound, until I was near the tree line then resumed my position near the trail, as if nothing had happened. I tried to look bored when I heard her coming.

Her hair was wet, and she had changed dresses. "Thanks Billy," she said.

"Uh, sure," I managed to say.

"I feel so much better."

So do I, I thought.

We walked slowly back toward the house. Nothing was said at first, but when we were halfway home she asked, "You saw me, didn't you, Billy?" Her voice was light and playful, and I didn't want to lie.

"Yes," I said.

"That's okay. I'm not mad."

"You're not?"

"No, I guess it's only natural, you know, for boys to look at girls."

It certainly seemed natural to me. I could think of nothing to say.

She continued. "If you'll go with me to the creek the next time, and be my lookout, then you can do it again."

"Do what again?"

"Watch me."

"Okay," I said, a little too quickly.
"But you can't tell anybody. It'll be our secret."
"I won't."

Over supper, I picked at my food and tried to behave as if nothing happened. It was difficult eating, though, with my stomach still turning flips. I could see Jessie just as clearly as if we were still at the creek.

I'd done a terrible thing. And I couldn't wait to do it again.

Wolf Creek near base of Tiger Mountain

Chapter 4

I met Richard Williams when I enrolled in school. He was a few months older than I was. Once in a while, on a Sunday afternoon, he would bring his rifle and I would take my father's 22, and we would hunt rabbits and squirrels. Richard became one of my best friends. Of course, there was Boots, Jessie, Sonny and Wilbur.

It was mid August before we chopped the last of the cotton. Grandma and Amon were going back to Muskogee where they lived. She asked my mother if she could take me and Ed to spend a week or two with her before school started. My mother was reluctant to let us go, but finally my father said, "Let the boys go. They have earned a vacation. They can swim in the pool at Honor Park and have a big time."

Ed and I were so excited. We caught the Motor Coach on Saturday. It went through Hitchita, Checotah, and then on to Muskogee. We only had to walk about a quarter of a mile to my grandmother's house on D Street.

The next day Grandma sewed bathing suits for us, and went with us to Honor Park to swim. I had never seen a swimming pool before. It even had a diving board. It was a far cry from Shorty's Pond, or the river. I had never worn a bathing suit before. There were a lot of kids in the pool. Ed and I showed off a little with our dives and such. We would swim here almost every day for a week.

The time passed quickly, and it was time to catch the Motor Coach back home. My parents met us at the Depot and took us home.

"You boys have a good time?" my father asked.

"We sure did," Ed said.

"Maybe we can go back again next summer," I stated.

"We'll see," my mother said. She had spent the week canning vegetables.

"Is Mr. Nolan and his family still here," I asked. "I didn't see any of them when we passed their house."

"Yes, they want to pick cotton for us this fall. I told them they could stay in the two-room shack until cotton picking was over."

"But I didn't see any of them around their place."

"They're probably down on the river fishing. They love those Carp and Catfish."

"I missed you boys, I'm so glad you're home," momma said.

"We missed you too." Ed and I answered at the same time.

We had just finished lunch when we heard a car coming up our road by the creek.

"I wonder who that could be," my mother said, as we walked to the front porch. A shiny black car pulled up in front of our house. "Oh my goodness, it's the McCollum's."

The McCollum's were my parent's best friends when we lived in California. I remembered playing with their daughter Patsy. She could contort her body into unusual positions. As I remember, she did acrobatics and was very flexible.

There were hugs and laughter as my parents greeted them.

"Charlie, it's good to see you and Rhoda. And look how much your boys have grown. Patsy has been anxious to see Edward and Billy again."

"What brings you to Oklahoma?" my father asked.

"We're on our way to visit relatives in Tennessee," Mr. McCollum said. "Rhoda gave us directions to your place in her last letter, so we thought we'd stop by and visit you on our way east."

"Well, it's sure good to see you and your family," my father stated.

While the adults were visiting, Ed and I showed Patsy the farm animals.

"You're as pretty as ever, Patsy," Ed said with a grin.

I thought she was pretty as well, but I was too bashful to say that. Ed tried to impress Patsy by chinning himself on the clothes line pole. I knew he was showing off. I could have done the same thing, but I played it cool. Patsy showed us her acrobatic skills by bending backward with her hands touching the ground, and then continued curling with her head up between her legs looking at us. It was the weirdest thing I'd ever seen. We talked about the good times we had playing together in California until it was time for them to leave.

We said our goodbyes and waved until they were out of sight.

Billy, Patsy, her little brother, and Ed.
The well house is behind us.

It was time to enroll in school again. Ed and I had birthdays in August. I was now eight and in the third grade. At the end of August the community came together at the school house for a pie supper to raise money for the school. The girls would bake pies to be auctioned off to the highest bidder. And whoever got the winning bid would eat the pie with the girl who made it.

There was a girl in our class that Richard and I both wanted to impress. She was a pretty blonde headed girl named Charlene Walling. Both Richard and I wanted to bid on her pie. The bidding started. One dollar, two dollars, it kept going higher. I had made eighteen dollars that summer, and I was determined to get her pie and impress her with my wealth. But Richard kept topping my bid. Finally, I said, "I bid Eighteen dollars."

Richard looked at his mother and she nodded to him. "Nineteen dollars," he said.

I was devastated. That was all the money I had. Richard won the bid and would sit with her while eating her pie. I walked outside and had a good cry. I said to myself, I didn't want her old pie anyway. I still had my money and two girl friends, Boots and Jessie. Richard had only one, besides, Charlene's mother probably made the pie anyway.

Bartlett School turned out at the beginning of cotton picking season. The break started the Monday following the community wide pie supper.

The Nolan family was still with us, and Grandma and Amon were back. That would be thirteen counting me and my brother.

My father had to purchase several extra cotton sacks. Some were nine, and some were ten feet long. The cotton wagon was parked at the far end of the cotton field. That end would be picked first, because if the rains came, that end would flood first. When a picker's sack was full, it would be weighed, recorded in a ledger, and then dumped into the cotton wagon.

On Monday my father stayed in the cotton field most of the day picking in different sections of the field to be certain that it was ready for picking. It was getting late in the day, and the sun was casting long shadows from the trees. Mom sent me to find my father.

I walked barefoot along a dirt path. The soil was dark and rich, good river bottom farm land that produced enough to keep you tied to it. Ahead I saw the cotton trailer and I knew he was working his way to it.

I stopped at the cotton trailer. It sat at the end of the cotton rows waiting to be filled. I climbed up on it. Around me, on all sides, neat rows of green and brown stalks stretched to the tree line. All over each stalk, puffy bolls of cotton were popping forth. The cotton was coming to life by the minute, so when I stepped on the back of the trailer and surveyed the field, I saw an ocean of white. The field was silent. No voices, no noise. For a moment, hanging on to the trailer, I could almost understand why my father wanted to be a farmer.

I could barely see his old straw hat in the distance as he moved between rows. I jumped down and ran to meet him. Because the sun and rain had cooperated, the leaves were full and thick and weaving together so that they brushed against me as I quickly made my way toward my father.

"Is that you Billy?" he called, knowing full well that it was me.

"Yes sir!" I answered, moving to the voice. "Mom says it's time to quit!"

"Oh she does?"

"Yes sir." The cotton was my height, and I missed him by one row. I cut through the stalks, and there he was, bent at the waist, both hands moving through the leaves, quickly plucking the cotton and stuffing it into the nearly full sack draped over his shoulder. He'd been in the field most of the day.

At the trailer, he lifted the strap of the cotton sack and hung it over the bottom of the scales. Then he lifted the bottom end of the sack that had a green boll inside the corner, wrapped with bailing wire with a loop on it to hang with the strap. The needle settled on sixty-eight pounds. He scribbled this on a ragged old ledger wired to the trailer.

"How much?" I asked when he closed the book.

"Four hundred-seventy."

"That's a lot of picking."

He shrugged and said, "not bad." He squatted and said, "Hop on."

I jumped on his back, and we started for the house. His shirt and overalls were soaked with sweat, and had been all day, but his arms were like steel.

One of my chores that morning was to fill a washtub half full of water and leave it in the sun all day so there'd be warn water for my father.

My mother was waiting for us by the side of the house. My father sat on a bench and removed his boots and socks. Then he unsnapped his overalls and took off his shirt. My mother dipped a hand towel in the tub and gently rubbed his neck with it.

"Billy," he said. "Run over to the Nolan's and tell them we'll be pickin' cotton tomorrow. Tell them to meet us here at 6:00 O'clock in the morning."

"Don't stay there and play with Wilbur and Sonny," my mother said. "Supper is about ready."

"Yes ma'am." I didn't say anything, but I was thinking, it's not Wilbur and Sonny I wanted to see. It was my precious Jessie.

After 75 years or so, the trees have grown up where we had cotton. Our old house was located just to the right of this picture.

This old house would be similar to ours in 1940

THE SON OF A SHARECROPPER

Road leads to the river bottom where we lived. This is where you go up and over the railroad tracks. The iron rails and Depot are long gone.

The road going up Bartlett Hill as it looks today. In 1940 it was much different. It was a clay road with deep ruts and deep ditches

The old bridge over Coal Creek west of
Wilson's store in Bartlett, Oklahoma.

Part Two

The Cotton Patch

A TIME TO REMEMBER

Chapter 5

At some point in the darkness of the night, my father, our human alarm clock, awoke, put on his boots, and began stomping around the kitchen making the first pot of coffee. The house was small—two bedrooms, a kitchen, a living room—and it was so old the plank floors sagged in places. If one person chose to wake up the rest, he or she could certainly do it.

My brother and I were allowed to stay in bed until my father came after us. Ed and I dressed quickly and met him outside the house.

The dew soaked our bare feet as we walked across the back yard. We stopped at the hen house. I slipped inside gathering eggs in the darkness from the day before. I was a little apprehensive, because last month I had killed a huge black snake that was coiled above the nests.

We then went to the barn where our jersey cow, Lucy, was waiting. I could milk the cow, but on most mornings that chore belonged to Ed. But my father was in a hurry because we had to be in the field by sunrise. He rapidly milked two gallons, which would have taken me half the morning. We delivered milk and eggs to the kitchen where the women were in charge. Fresh side bacon was already in the cast iron skillet, its rich aroma thick in the air.

We put our milk and other perishables in a wire basket and lowered it in our well just above the water to keep them cool. The following year, my father purchased a used oak ice box. Whenever we went to town, we would pick up a fifty pound block of ice from the Henryetta Ice Plant. This made my mother happy.

Breakfast was fresh eggs, salt-cured side bacon, with hot biscuits and sorghum. As they cooked, I settled into my chair, ran my fingers over the damp checkered oil cloth, and waited for my first cup of coffee. It was the one vice my mother allowed my grandmother to give us boys.

Grandma placed the cup and saucer before me, then the sugar bowl and fresh cream. I doctored the coffee until it was as sweet as a malt, then poured some in a saucer to cool it like Amon did.

At breakfast, conversation in the kitchen was held to a minimum. It was exciting to have pickers on our farm for the harvest, but the enthusiasm was dampened by the reality that we would spend most of the next twelve hours unshielded by the sun, bent over, picking until our fingers bled.

We ate quickly, the roosters making a ruckus in the side yard. Grandma's biscuits were perfectly round, and so warm that when I carefully placed a glob of butter in the center of one, it melted instantly. I watched the yellow cream soak into the biscuit, then took a bite. My mother conceded that Minnie made the best biscuits she'd ever tasted. I wanted so badly to eat two or three, like my father, but I simply couldn't hold them. I was as full as a tick, as Grandma would say. My mother ate one, same with Grandma. Ed ate two, Dad and Amon had three. Several hours later, in the middle of the morning, we would stop for a few minutes beside the cotton trailer to eat the leftover biscuits.

After breakfast there had been some chatter about the weather as we listened to the news on our Philco battery powered radio.

My father had been reading the almanac and offered the opinion that the weather would cooperate throughout most of the month of September. But mid-October looked ominous. Bad weather would come. The harder we worked, the harder the Nolan's would work. This was my father's version of a pep talk.

When my father finished his last bite, he thanked his mother and mom for the good breakfast and left them to clean up the mess. I strutted onto the front porch with the men. Our house faced the north, the cotton field to the east. The corn patch was across the creek to the west. My father and the Nolan's had already shocked the corn.

I saw the first hint of orange peeking through the trees that lined the bank of the Deep Fork River. The sun was coming up, undaunted by clouds.

The Nolan family met us at the front of the house. The mules had been hitched to the wagon, and everybody got in.

My father spoke to the Nolan family. "Good morning. Are you ready to work?"

I walked around to the mules checking their harness, trying my best to impress you know who. But my haughtiness, however, would vanish shortly, because all things were level among the cotton stalks.

Without a word my father popped the reins and the wagon lurched forward. I stood at the back of the wagon seat looking to see if anyone fell off. Through the kitchen window I could see my mother watching us as she cleaned the dishes. She would finish her chores, spend a while in the garden, and then join us for a hard day in the field. No one rested when the cotton was ready.

The Sun rising on another hot day in the cotton patch

In a few minutes we arrived at the cotton trailer. Before I jumped down, I noticed the sky was coming to life with streaks of orange and yellow. There wasn't a cloud to be seen. It also meant no shelter from the scorching sun.

Jessie said, "Good morning, Billy," as she walked by. I managed to return her greeting. She smiled at me as if she knew some secret that she would never tell.

"Choose a row and start pickin'," my father said.

Without a word the Nolan's draped their long cotton sacks over their shoulders, selected a row and began picking.

For a second, I stood there staring down a very long, straight row of cotton, a row that had somehow been assigned to me. I thought, I'll never get to the end of it, and I was suddenly tired. The one thing that motivated me, however, I had my father on the row beside me. He did not tolerate laziness. Second, I longed for a Red Rider BB gun that I had seen in the Sears Roebuck Catalog in the Out House. I tore that page out and hid it so nobody would use it for you know what. I got paid for pickin', same as the others. A dollar per one hundred pounds, and I had big plans for that money.

"Let's go," my father yelled firmly in Ed's direction. He and Sonny were talking and had not yet started. My father was already settled into the stalks, ten feet into a row. My brother sang as he moved down his row. He was a dreamer, but the cotton patch was not a part of his dream world.

It was not uncommon to hear Jim and Mammy Nolan singing, as they picked. Jessie laughed about something, her luxurious voice echoed across the field. I had just turned eight years of age, and now she was only seven years older than I was. And I thought, yeah, it could work.

With solemn resolve, I flung my nine-foot cotton sack across my back, the strap over my shoulder, and attacked the first boll of cotton. I picked as fast as possible, with both hands, and stuffed the cotton into the sack. I had to be careful though, my father would inspect my row at some point during the morning. If I left too much cotton in the bolls, then I would be reprimanded.

As deftly as I could, I worked my small hands through the maze of stalks, grabbing the cotton, avoiding if possible the sharp burrs because they were pointed and could draw blood. I bobbed and weaved and inched along, falling farther behind my father.

Our cotton was so thick that the stalks from each row intertwined. They were as tall as I was. They brushed against my face. After the incident with the black snake a few weeks ago, I watched every step around the farm, especially in the cotton field. I'd seen plenty of Copperhead and Cottonmouth snakes, especially near the creeks and river.

Before long I was all alone, a child left behind by those with quicker hands and stronger backs. I took comfort, however, because Ed and Sonny were farther back than I was. The Sun was a bright orange ball, rising fast into position to sear the land for another day. When my father was out of sight, I decided to take my first break. Jessie was the nearest person. She was five rows over and fifty feet ahead of me. I could barely see her faded denim bonnet above the cotton.

My father had planted by hand a watermelon seed every hundred feet or so on about every ten rows. I had come to one of the vines. It had two watermelons on it. I thumped one—dead ripe. I busted it open and grabbed a chunk of its heart and enjoyed the sweetness of its taste. Then I stretched out on my cotton sack, which after an hour was depressingly flat. There were a few soft lumps, but nothing significant. I'd been expected to pick a hundred pounds a day, and since I was now eight years of age, my fear was that my quota was about to increase.

Lying on my back, I watched through the stalks the perfectly clear sky, hoped for clouds, and dreamed of a BB gun. Every August we received by mail the latest edition of the Sears, Roebuck Catalog, and few events were more momentous, at least in my life. It came in a brown wrapper, all the way from Chicago, and was required by my mother to be kept next to the radio. The old one would be taken to the outhouse for another purpose.

On page 305 of the current catalog was an incredible ad for a Red Rider BB gun. It cost $7.95 plus shipping. Two weeks of hard labor and I'd have enough money to purchase one. My father thought it was a waste of money, but I could tell he secretly admired it.

"Billy!" a stern voice shot through the stillness of the field. Stalks were snapping nearby.

"Yes sir," I said, jumping to my feet, thrusting my hands at the nearest bolls of cotton.

My father was suddenly standing over me. "What are you doing?" he asked.

"I had to pee," I said, without stopping my hands.

"It took you a long time," he said, unconvinced.

"Yes sir. It's all that coffee." I looked up at him. He knew the truth.

"Try to keep up," he said, turning around and walked away.

"Yes sir," I said to him, knowing I could never keep up with him.

He turned back around and yelled at Ed. "Quit loafing around. We have cotton to pick."

Just as he turned to walk away, I saw a snake slithering slowly up my row.

"Snake!" I shouted. "It's a copperhead!"

My father turned and rushed back. He quickly grabbed the snake by its tail, twirled it around his head a couple of times and snapped the snake like a whip. It popped, and the head of the snake was dangling by a thread.

"Wow!" I said, totally amazed.

"Don't you boys ever try that," my father said. "It's very dangerous."

Back in April, my father had just finished plowing when a cottontail rabbit jumped up in front of him. He chased the rabbit. The rabbit outran him for the first hundred yards, but then he started gaining on the rabbit. Having run perhaps a quarter mile, the rabbit became exhausted. My father caught the rabbit by the hind legs, and hit it behind the head to kill it. My daddy was a superman. I loved my daddy. We had rabbit for supper that night.

A ten-foot sack like the adults used held about sixty to seventy pounds of cotton, so by nine O'clock they were ready to weigh. My father was in charge of the scales, which hung from the end of the trailer. The sacks were hoisted up and hung on the scales. The needle sprang around like the long handle of a large clock. Everyone could see how much each person picked. Then the cotton sack was shoved even higher and emptied into the trailer. No time for a rest. You caught the sack when it was tossed down. You went back where you were picking or started another row for another couple of hours.

I was in the middle of an endless row of cotton, sweating, boiling in the sun, bending over, trying to be fast with my hands, and stopping occasionally to see where my father was so that maybe I could arrange another nap. But there was never an opportunity to drop my sack. Instead, I plowed ahead, working hard, waiting for the sack to get heavy, and wondering for the first time if I really needed a BB gun.

After an eternity in the field, I heard my father snap a command to the mules, and I knew it was time for lunch. Though I had not completed my first row, I didn't really care.

I drug my sack to the scales, where my father whirled it around over his shoulder as if it were empty, and quickly weighed it. All that back-numbing labor for thirty-nine pounds of cotton.

We all headed for the house. Lunch was at noon sharp. My mother and Grandma had left the field an hour earlier to prepare it.

That afternoon I left my cotton sack where I was picking and walked back to the wagon for some water. I found Ed and Sonny sitting under the wagon in the shade. Mammy Nolan's snuff box, a little round metal container, was sitting on top of the coupling pole.

"I dare you to take a dip," Sonny said to Ed.

"You go first," Ed said.

Sonny took the lid off, reared back, opened his mouth and said, "It won't come out."

Ed reached up and tapped the bottom of the snuff container and a big glob turned loose and covered his face. Sonny was choking, trying to get his breath, coughing and screaming.

I looked up and saw Mammy Nolan running toward us, the cotton bolls flying. She was a big woman. I had heard my father say to my mother that Mammy Nolan was two axe handles across the butt, and top heavy. We both ran toward the creek and hid. We never did know how that episode ended.

After a while, we sneaked back to our cotton sacks as if nothing happened. At six O'clock we weighed up and headed for the house.

A chore I dreaded after all day in the cotton patch, was in the garden. I thought it was cruel to force me, or any other eight year old kid for that matter, to awake before sunrise, work in the field all day, and then pull garden duty before supper. But I knew we were lucky to have such a beautiful garden.

My mother loved this little plot of soil because it was hers—no one else really wanted it. She treated it like a sanctuary. It fed her family. When the house was crowded, I could always find her in the garden, talking to her vegetables. When harsh words were spoken, I knew my mother would disappear into her refuge.

I could hardly carry my bucket by the time she'd finished her selections. Things like cucumbers, tomatoes, squash, bell peppers, onions and such.

Of an evening after supper we would sit on the front porch, Grandma and my mother on one side shelling peas, my father and Amon on the other side talking about the price of cotton. Ed and I sat on the edge of the porch with our feet dangling off it, waiting for the heat to relent so we could go to bed without sweating.

Lying on our pallet, I would kick off the sheet so I could breath. I listened to the crickets and locust, sing their screeching chorus, calling to each other. They serenaded us every night in the summer, and I dreamed of my beloved Jessie.

We gathered at the wagon the next morning. Everyone was in a daze, eyes half opened and down cast, dreading another day of sun and drudgery. The wagon rocked and swayed as we slowly made our way into the field. I gazed at the field of cotton and tried to picture my shiny Red Rider BB gun, just like the one in the Sears Roebuck catalog. It never failed to inspire me, but the wagon stopped, and all I could see was the looming cotton, just standing there, row after row, waiting.

The work almost killed me during the afternoon. Late in the day I limped toward the cotton trailer, lugging my harvest behind me, hot and thirsty, soaked with sweat, my fingers swollen from the tiny shallow punctures inflicted by the sharp, needle-like burrs. I already had forty-one pounds for the day, and I was certain I had at least thirty pounds in my sack. I was hoping my mother would be somewhere near the scales because she would insist that I be allowed to quit and go to the house.

Only my father was allowed to weigh the cotton, and if he happened to be deep in a row somewhere, then you got a break while he worked his way back to the trailer. I didn't see him, so the idea of a nap floated before me.

Jessie, her older and younger sisters, along with Sonny had gathered at the end of the trailer in the shade. They were sitting on their bulky cotton sacks, resting.

Cotton Pickers

weighing cotton

I freed myself from the shoulder strap of my cotton sack and walked to the end of the trailer.

"Howdy," Sonny said.

"Howdy," I answered.

Jessie was sitting next to her sisters. Her oldest sister never smiled. It seemed to me that she frowned all the time. She was nothing like Jessie.

"You got anything to eat boy?" the older sister asked, her eyes flashing at me. For a second I was too surprised to say anything. Jessie just shook her head and studied the ground.

"Do you?" she demanded, shifting her weight so that she faced me squarely.

"Uh, no," I managed to say.

"You mean 'No ma'am' don't you boy? She said angrily.

"Come on, Jamie," Jessie said. The rest of them seemed to withdraw. Their heads were bowed.

"No ma'am," I said. I was shocked.

"No ma'am what?" Her voice was sharper.

"No ma'am," I said again.

"You farm folks are right uppity, you know that? You think you're better than us black folks cause you have this farm and cause you pay us to work it. Ain't that right, boy?"

"That's enough Jamie," Jessie said.

I suddenly hoped my father would appear. I was ready for her to leave our farm.

My lower lip began to tremble. I was hurt and embarrassed and didn't know what to say. I was on the verge of tears, so I turned and ran past the trailer and along the field road until I was safely out of sight. Then I ducked into the cotton and waited for friendly voices. I sat on the hot ground, surrounded by stalks of cotton over five feet tall, and I cried, something I really hated to do. I would tell nobody. It would have to be another secret to keep.

I decided I would simply avoid Jamie until the picking was over and they went back to Grayson. At some point later in the winter when we sat around the pot bellied stove in the living room and told stories about the harvest, I would finally serve up Jamie's misdeeds. I'd have plenty of time to work on my stories, and would embellish where I deemed appropriate. It was a Spencer tradition.

It was finally Saturday morning. At sunrise, we were all in the cotton field. I kept close to my father, for fear that monster Jamie might come after me again. She ignored me. I hope she was ashamed of herself.

I was half asleep, not paying attention to anything in particular, when the sweetest voice said, "Good morning, Billy." It was Jessie, just standing there smiling at me. It was her way of saying she was sorry for the other day.

Because I was a Spencer, I was capable of deep stubbornness. I turned my back to her and walked away. I attacked the first row of cotton as if I might wipe out forty acres before lunch. After a few minutes, though, I was tired. I was lost in the stalks in the dark, and I could still hear her sweet voice and see her smile.

We didn't go to town every Saturday, especially, during the cotton picking and chopping time, but when we did go, it was a treat. We'd work half a day, eat lunch, clean up, and head for town. Ed and I would get to see a movie at the Morgan or Blaine Theaters. The show cost ten cents, and a nickel for popcorn or a soda pop. You could save the empty bottles and trade them back to the store for a penny each. We were fortunate. A lot of sharecroppers seldom left the farm. They didn't have the money for groceries, or a car to get to town.

The Saturday bath was a ritual I hated more than picking cotton. It took place after lunch, under the stern supervision of my mother. The tub, hardly big enough for my brother, was used later in the day by other members of the family. It was kept at the back side of the house.

First, I had to haul the water from the well house where I would fill the tub about half full. This task took about six trips with a bucket, and I was exhausted before the bath began. Then I stripped naked with remarkable speed.

With a bar of home-made soap and a washcloth, I worked furiously to make bubbles and otherwise cloud the water so my mother couldn't see my privates when she came to direct matters. She appeared first to collect my dirty clothes, then to bring a clean change. Then she went straight for the ears and neck. In her hands the washcloth became a weapon. She scrapped my tender skin as if the soil I collected working in the field offended her. Throughout the process, she continued to marvel at how dirty I could get.

When my neck was raw, she attacked my hair as if it were filled with lice. She poured water from a bucket over my head to rinse off the soap. My humiliation was complete when she finished scouring my arms and legs—mercifully, she left the midsection for me.

The water was muddy when I hopped out—a week's worth of dirt collected from the Deep Fork River Bottom. I dumped the water, toweled off, and stepped into my clean overalls. I felt fresh and clean and five pounds lighter, and I was ready for town.

I loved the traffic and the crowded sidewalks on any given Saturday in Henryetta. We waited as a car backed out of a parking space about a block from the Doe Boy statue that stood in the middle of Main Street. It was placed there to honor the veterans of WW 1.

There was a den of noise as people chatted with friends or relatives. Some of the men who came to town would head for the pool hall. The women gathered in such places as the grocery store, or sit in their cars and watch the people milling together visiting. Gladys Williams called it 'People-Watching.' Actually, watching people can be quite interesting.

I followed my mother into the grocery store. Ed had gone to the Barber Shop. He told me he was going to ask for a job shining shoes. I suspected he was trying to get out of picking cotton.

The store was packed with mostly women.

"Well, hello Billy," she said as she winked at me. It was mom's best friend, Gladys. "How's the cotton?" she asked. It was the same question you heard over and over.

"Pickin' well," I said, as if I'd hauled in a ton.

It took mom an hour to buy five pounds of flour, five pounds of sugar, two pounds of coffee, a bottle of vinegar, and a pound of table salt. The aisles were crowded with women more concerned with visiting than buying food. They talked about their gardens, the weather, and who was having a baby, and who might be. They prattled about a funeral here, or an upcoming wedding.

My only chore was to carry the groceries back to the car. When this was accomplished, I was free to roam until four O'clock. That's when the movie started. Some of the movie attractions to come were: Gene Autry, Hop-A-Long Cassidy, and the Lone Ranger. My mother and Gladys would go back to the car where they could visit in private and be entertained by watching people.

With the groceries delivered to our car, I roamed through the crowd and found my hunting partner, Richard, Gladys' son.

"Whatcha doin'?" I asked.

"Just waitin' for the movie to start," he said. "Been huntin' lately?"

"Yep," I answered. "I Killed me three rabbits and two squirrels last Sunday."

"I would go huntin' with you, but I guess you're too busy with the cotton."

"Come some Sunday, and we'll get us some rabbits."

We decided to get us some ice cream at the drug store, and as we were walking down the street, we passed their car with mom and his mother in it. They called us over to the car.

"Where you boys goin'," Gladys asked.

"We thought we would get us an ice cream cone," Richard answered.

"Your movie starts in a little bit, so don't you boys go wondering off too far."

"We won't," Richard said.

Chapter 6

Sunday was a day of rest, but there were always chores to do.

Richard Williams came down to the house around nine O'clock Sunday morning. We had talked about going hunting the day before when we met for the movie in Henryetta.

"Which way you want to go, Billy?" he asked.

"Let's go over to Wolf Creek and make our way down the timber line. I'm sure we'll see squirrels, and maybe jump a rabbit or two."

As we made our way through the trees along the creek, we heard the chatter of a squirrel making a fuss about something. He was on the trunk of a cottonwood tree with his head toward the ground, popping his tail, and making a lot of noise.

"There must be something at the foot of that tree," I told Richard. "Let's sneak a little closer to get a better look."

We moved quietly to a better position. At the base of the tree was a coiled Cottonmouth snake, with its head perhaps a foot above its body, weaving back and forth.

"Would you look at the size of that snake," Richard whispered. "I've never seen one that big. His body is the size of my arm."

"That's why the squirrel is disturbed," I said.

We watched as the squirrel got closer and closer to the base of the tree, fussing and popping its tail. When it was a couple of feet from the ground, the snake struck quickly, sinking its fangs into the squirrel. After a few seconds, the squirrel's body went limp.

I took dead aim with my 22 rifle and blew the snakes head off. The snake measured seven feet long. I knew that Cottonmouth snakes are poisonous, so we left the squirrel where it lay with the snake.

Two hours later, we were back at the house with two rabbits and two squirrels. Richard didn't want the game we killed, so I cleaned them for our family to eat. After lunch, Richard went home.

That afternoon, Jim Nolan came to the house. The Sunday before, my father and Jim had started building a fish net. Dad had cut some green willow saplings to use as hoops, and chicken wire for the throat and covering. The hoops were not perfectly round, but it would work. It looked a little whopper jawed, as Grandma would say. When they were finished, my father hung a bag of sour feed in it, put it in the wagon, hooked the mules to the wagon and made our way to one of three natural lakes in the river bottom, Flag Lake, Horseshoe Lake, and Snag Lake. We chose Snag Lake. My father and Jim carried it from the wagon into about three feet of water.

The next evening, after our work in the cotton, we all walked down to the lake to see if we had any fish, including Sonny and Wilbur.

The trap was about seven or eight feet long and three feet in diameter. Dad got on the back end of the trap and Jim on the front with his back to the trap, lifted it, and began carrying it to dry ground. As they walked into shallower water, the fish began flopping. Jim yelled, "Challee, we gonna have fish tonight." Then, looking back over his shoulder to get a good look at the fish, he saw four or five Cottonmouth snakes with their heads pushed through the chicken wire. Jim screamed and dropped the trap. He ran out of the water yelling back at Dad, "Challee! Challee! get away from thar man! One a them snakes bite ya, you'd die befo God got the news!"

Sonny and Ed helped my father get the trap out of the water. We killed the snakes and took the fish out of the trap. The snakes were so full of fish that they couldn't escape through the wire mesh.

After a few weeks in the cotton patch, I was glad to go back to school. However, my brother and I were still expected to pick cotton after school. We would run home, change clothes, pick up our cotton sacks, and pick cotton until almost dark.

The trailer had a tarp to hold the cotton and keep it from blowing onto the road leading to the gin. Our old tarp was tied firmly in place, securing the fruit of our labor, one hundred and fifty pounds had been picked by me over the last couple of days. My father had never taken a load to the gin with cotton flying out like snow and littering the road side. Other folks did, though, and the ditches along the highway had slowly grown white as farmers hurried to the gin with their harvest.

With the loaded cotton trailer dwarfing Mr. Wilson's borrowed pickup, Dad drove less than twenty miles per hour on the way to town.

I counted seven trailers ahead of us when we arrived at the gin. Another dozen or so sat empty and parked to one side. Those could leave one to be ginned at night while the other stayed in the field. My father desperately wanted a second trailer.

My father parked and walked to a group of farmers huddled by a trailer. I could tell by the way they were standing that they were worried about something, perhaps the price of cotton going down.

The parking area was crowded with cotton trailers, some empty, others waiting for their harvest to be ginned. I waved at some boys in the bed of a truck, pulling an empty trailer, headed home for another load.

For nine months the gin sat idle. It was a tall, long box-like structure. In early September it came to life when the harvest began. At the height of picking season it ran all day and night, stopping only on Saturday night and Sunday morning.

The Farmers Gin roared with the chorus of heavy machines at work that could be heard throughout the town. They were incredibly loud and dangerous. During each picking season, at least one would fall victim to some gruesome injury inside the cotton gin. I was scared of the machines, and when my father told me to wait outside, I was happy to do so.

I found a safe spot near the dock, where they wheeled out the finished bales and loaded them onto trailers.

A bale of cotton was worth a hundred and twenty-five dollars, give or take, depending on the markets. A good crop could produce a bale an acre. We sharecropped forty acres. Most farm kids could do the math. In fact, the math was so easy you wondered why anyone would want to be a farmer.

Farmers Gin located just across the
railroad tracks on East Trudgeon

My mother made sure we understood the numbers. She never intended for her boys to stay on the farm.

Most farmers borrowed money from the owner of the gin. That was their crop loan, and the money was spent on seed, fertilizer, labor, and other expenses. So far we had been lucky. The weather had been perfect, and the crop looked good. If our luck continued through the picking and the field yielded a bale an acre, then the Spencer farming operation would break even. That was our goal.

When we left the gin, my father had nothing to say. The wrinkles on his forehead were closer together, and his chin jutted out a bit, so I knew he'd heard bad news. I assumed it had something to do with the price of cotton.

I said nothing as we left Henryetta. With the town behind us, I cocked my head toward the open window to catch the wind. The air was hot, and I wanted my father to drive faster so we could cool off. When I looked over at the speedometer; thirty miles per hour.

We woke up on Sunday morning with a rumble of thunder and rain. A storm blew in from the northwest. I wondered why it rained on Sunday. Why not through the week, so I wouldn't have to pick cotton. Sunday was already a day of rest.

The rain poured down, as if to make up for two weeks or so of dry weather. My father was on the porch, watching the storm and gazing into the distance at the river, no doubt beginning to worry that floodwaters were coming.

We only had half of the cotton picked. If the river bottom flooded, it would wipe us out. I felt sorry for my father.

My father had planted five acres of peanuts near the house and along the creek. Water was standing between the rows. He thought that peanuts would be a good cash crop.

It rained off and on all day, as we listened to the radio for weather reports. There was talk among the adults of the possibility of a flood. However, late in the day the rain stopped, and I could see a break in the clouds.

The next day after school, Max Wilson and his brothers Ervin and Leroy, along with Richard and Roy Williams decided to walk with me and Ed down the railroad track to the river. Someone had told Max that the river was almost out of its banks, and we all agreed to see it.

We left the railroad track, which was near the highway bridge. We wanted to look down at the swift moving water from the bridge. There was no traffic. There was a lot of trash in the fast moving, muddy water, tree limbs, brush, and an occasional log.

Max dared us to strip and jump into the water from the bridge. "I'll go, if everybody goes," Ervin challenged.

All agreed. Ervin stripped off his clothes and jumped, barely missing a log partially submerged. The swift water took him down the river as he angled toward the muddy bank.

"Who's next?" Max asked.

"I'll go," I stated bravely. Our mother had warned us to never swim in the river without our father present. But this looked like fun. I jumped off the bridge into the muddy water. My head came out of the water thirty or forty feet down stream. I swam at an angle to the bank. As I was getting out, Leroy jumped, then Richard, Ed, and Max. Roy did not.

"I'll bring your clothes to you," Roy yelled.

We put on our clothes, even though we were wet. We made our way to the railroad track and headed for Bartlett. About a half mile or so up the tracks, Ed and I left the others and made our way home.

Our mother was waiting. She knew that we should have been home long before now. "Where have you boys been?" she demanded.

"Uh, playing," Ed answered.

"Look at your clothes! Your eyes are blood shot. Have you boys been swimming in the river?"

"Um, yes ma'am," we both admitted, looking down at our muddy feet.

"You boys disobeyed me. It's a wonder you didn't drown. Ed, run to the creek and cut me a switch. You boys deserve a whippin'. She kept her word, and I thought she would never stop. I tried not to cry, but I did.

It was three days before we could pick cotton again. I didn't mind. I enjoyed the break from running home from school to pick cotton in the late afternoon.

Deep Fork River
The old bridge we jumped from when
the river was at flood stage

Chapter 7

We were eating breakfast early Saturday morning, and I was wondering if we would be going to town.

"Carnival's in town," Pappy said.

My fork froze in midair. "What time are we goin'?" I asked.

"Just after lunch," he said.

"How late can we stay," Ed asked.

"We'll see about that," he said.

The carnival hit the small farming towns in the fall, just when the harvest was winding down and folks had money in their pockets. They usually arrived on Thursday and set up on the baseball field, and stayed through the weekend. Nothing excited Henryetta like the carnival.

All carnivals had a Ferris wheel, a merry-go-round, and several other rides that squeaked and rattled and generally terrified all the mothers. The Slinger had been such a ride, a circle of swings on chains that went faster and faster, until the riders were flying parallel to the ground and screaming for it to stop. But folks lined up to ride it.

There were booths where you threw rings and darts and shot pellet pistols to win prizes. There were hawkers shouting their wares. They were loud and colorful with excitement. Word would spread quickly throughout the communities surrounding Henryetta, and people would flock into town, and in a few hours the town would be packed.

I was desperate to go. I choked down my biscuits and ran outside, anxious for noon to come. We would pick cotton till noon, clean up, and head for town.

"The carnival's in town," I whispered to Jessie, as we made our way to the field.

"You'll goin'?" she asked.

"Of course, nobody misses the carnival."

At noon we ate lunch quickly, then, hurried about the task of getting myself scrubbed and bathed. My mother knew my brother and I were anxious to get to town, so she wasted no time with her scouring.

Henryetta, when the Carnival was in town

Traffic on Main Street was already packed, the sidewalks crowded. We found a parking space down a side street, and everyone piled out. Grandma and my mother headed for the stores.

"Can I go to the carnival," I asked, as Ed took off in a run.

"Of course you can," my father said. "How much money do you have?"

"Five dollars."

"I think three is enough."

"How about four?"

"Make it three-fifty, okay?"

"Yes sir." I ran, darting through people, and was soon at the baseball field. The carnival covered it all. The Ferris wheel stood in the middle, surrounded by smaller rides, the booths, and the midway. Shrill music rattled from the loudspeakers on the merry-go-round. Long lines of people were already waiting. I could smell popcorn and corn dogs and something frying in grease.

I found the trailer with the cotton candy. It cost a dime, but I would have paid much more for it. Richard saw me at the midway as I watched some older boys shoot air guns at little ducks that swam in a pool. They never hit them, and this was because, according to my father, the gun sights were crooked.

We bought candied apples for ten cents and took our time inspecting the carnival. There was a witch in a long black dress, black hair, black everything, and for fifteen cents she could tell your fortune. The midway had the usual collection of games—softballs thrown at milk jugs, basketballs aimed at rims that were too small, darts at balloons, hoops over bottlenecks.

We strolled through the carnival, savoring the noise and excitement. A crowd was gathering at the far end of the field, and we drifted over. A large sign proclaimed the presence of "Samson, World's Greatest Wrestler, Direct from Egypt," and under it was a square mat with padded poles in the corners and ropes around it. Samson was not in the ring, but his appearance was only moments away, according to Delilah, a tall shapely woman with a microphone. Her costume revealed all of her legs and most of her chest, and I was certain that never before had so much skin been exposed in public in Henryetta. She explained to a silent crowd, mostly men, that the rules were simple. Samson paid ten-to-one to any person who could stay in the ring with him for one minute. "Only sixty seconds!" she yelled. "And the money is yours." Her accent was strange enough to convince us that they were indeed from another land. I'd never seen anybody from Egypt, though I knew from Grandma that Moses had had some adventures there.

She paraded back and forth in front of the ring, and all eyes were on every move. Music started blaring from a loud speaker hanging on the sign. "And now, ladies and gentlemen!" she shouted above the music, "I present to you, the one, the only, the greatest wrestler in all the world, the incredible Samson!"

I held my breath.

He bounded from behind a curtain and jumped into the ring amid tepid applause. Why should we clap for him? He was there to whip us. His hair was the first thing I noticed. It was black and fell to his shoulders like a woman's. He was a giant of a man, with a thick body and ridges of muscles. His arms were covered with black hair and looked strong enough to lift buildings. He strutted around the ring in step with the music, curling his arms and flexing his muscles.

"Who's first?" Delilah yelled into the microphone as the music died. "Two dollars minimum!"

The crowd was suddenly still. Only a fool would crawl into that ring.

"I ain't scared," somebody yelled, and we watched in disbelief at a young man I'd never seen before stepped forward and handed two dollars to Delilah. She took the money and said, "Ten-to-one. Stay in the ring for sixty seconds, and you'll win twenty dollars." She shoved the microphone at the young man and said, "What's your name?"

"George."

"Good luck George."

He climbed into the ring as if he had no fear of Samson, who'd been watching without the slightest hint of worry. Delilah struck a bell on the side of the ring. "Sixty seconds!" she said.

George moved around a bit, then, retreated to a corner as Samson took a step in his direction.

"Forty-five seconds!" she called out.

Samson moved closer and George darted to the other side of the ring. Being much smaller, he was also much quicker, and apparently was using the strategy of flight. Samson stalked him. George kept darting.

"Thirty seconds!"

The ring was not big enough to run much, and Samson tripped George during one of his sprints. He picked George up and wrapped an arm tightly around the boy's head.

"Twenty seconds!"

Samson twisted his prey and grimaced with sadistic pleasure, while poor George flailed at his side.

"Ten seconds!"

Samson whirled and flung George across the ring. Before George could get up, the World's Greatest Wrestler grabbed him by the foot, lifted him in the air, held him over the ropes, and with two seconds to go, dropped him to the ground for the victory.

George was in a daze, but he walked away in one piece and seemed to be proud of himself. He had proved his manhood, had shown no fear, and had come within two seconds of winning twenty bucks. I'd finally seen a worse job than picking cotton.

It was quite a spectacle, and Richard and I stood for some time watching Samson dispose of one victim after another. Samson was soaked with sweat and needed a break, so Richard and I scooted off to ride the Ferris wheel twice. We were debating whether to get another helping of cotton candy when we heard some young men talking about the girlie show.

"She takes off everything!" one of them said as he walked by, and we forgot about the cotton candy. We followed them to the end of the midway, where the gypsies' trailer was parked. Behind the trailer was a small tent that had obviously been erected so that no one would see it. A few men smoked and waited, and they all had a guilty look about them. There was music coming from the tent.

Richard and I didn't recognize any of the men hanging around the girlie tent. We circled through the trailers and flanked in from the opposite side, but a large dog had been chained to the ground, guarding against peeping toms like us. We retreated and decided to wait for darkness.

As four o'clock approached, we had to make a painful decision—to go to the matinee, or stay at the carnival. We stayed.

It was now almost dark. The air was filled with the sounds of the carnival; the excited screams of kids on the rides, the music shrieking forth from a dozen assorted speakers, the constant jabbering of barkers as they enticed folks to part with their money to win another prize. The people were so thick you couldn't stir them with a stick, as Grandma would say. Long lines snaked around the rides. I had never seen so many people in one place.

We found our parents near the street in the Williams car, watching the spectacle from a safe distance.

"How much money you got?" my father asked.
"Bout a dollar," I said.
"Have you seen Edward?" my mother asked.
"No, but I think he is with Bud Gaither."
"That Ferris wheel doesn't look safe, Richard," Gladys said.
"We've been on it twice. It's okay," Richard responded.
"I'll give each of you another dollar if you won't ride it again," Gladys offered.
"It's a deal," Richard said.

Gladys handed us a dollar a piece, and we agreed to check back with them in an hour. We decided that it was time to investigate the girlie show. We darted through the throng along the midway and slowed near the gypsies' trailer. It was much darker back there. In front of the tent were some men smoking cigarettes, and in the door was a young woman in a skimpy costume swinging her hips and dancing in a naughty way.

We sneaked along the shadows, advancing slowly until a strange voice from nowhere said, "That's far enough. You boys get out of here." We froze and looked around, and about that time we heard another voice yell behind us, "Repent, ye workers of iniquity! Repent!"

It was Reverend Robinson, Pastor of Dewar Baptist Church, standing tall with his Bible in one hand while a long, crooked finger pointed out from the fist of the other.

"You brood of vipers!" he yelled at the top of his lungs.

I don't know if the young lady stopped dancing or if the men scattered. We didn't bother to look. Richard and I hit the ground on all fours and crawled like hunted prey through the maze of trailers and trucks until we saw light between two of the booths on the midway. We emerged and got lost in the crowd.

Blaine Theater, Henryetta, Oklahoma

Morgan Theater, Henryetta, Oklahoma

THE SON OF A SHARECROPPER

Central Drug Store, Henryetta, Oklahoma.

The J.P. Martin Company Department Store, located at 509 West Main. G.A. Crockett was the manager.

The J.P. Martin Department Store located at
509 West Main. G.A. Crockett, mgr.

Browns printing company 500 block west Main. The
man on left is Francis Brown.
At right is employee John Crosby Jr. Picture
taken in 1941 when they opened.

THE SON OF A SHARECROPPER

Gas 12 cents a gallon, Kerosene 10 cents a gallon

Main Street Barber Shop, Henryetta, Oklahoma

Shoe Shine Chair in Main Barber Shop, Henryetta, Oklahoma, 2018
Ed Spencer shined shoes in this same chair, 1945-46

THE SON OF A SHARECROPPER

Main Street, Henryetta, Oklahoma

Inside Wholesale Grocery store, Henryetta, Oklahoma

Chapter 8

In early spring of 1940, when we moved from the two room house to the four room house, my father cut two forked limbs from a willow tree and made my brother and I a yoked slingshot. Some would call it a bean flip, others something else. We found two old red rubber inner tubes in the old tool shed and cut strips of rubber about a half inch wide and a foot long. He took a leather tongue from an old shoe for the pocket, and punched holes on each side of the leather to secure the rubber ends to it. He then stretched the other ends of the rubber over the fork ends and tied them off. It was a weapon I carried in my back pocket constantly.

Mrs. Conklin was a widow with three children. They lived about a quarter of mile or so west of us along Coal Creek. She had two boys, Luke, who was twenty-one, and Fred, nineteen. Boots was the youngest at twelve. My parents would often go visit Mrs. Conklin and play pitch. She had an older milk cow named Bess, and sold cream, butter, and eggs in town.

Because Boots lived in the river bottom, I saw her more often than my school friends in Bartlett. We would often go down to the creek, pick up some smooth stones and shoot turtles and snakes with my weapon. Even though she was older than I was, we were best buddies.

It was in late October before we finished with the cotton. My father, with the mules and turning plow, turned over the five acres of peanuts to expose the roots that had peanuts attached. Our job was to shake the soil from the peanuts and turn the plants upside down so the peanuts could dry out. My father had arranged for a threshing machine to come the following week.

The threshing machine was noisy as the crew threshed the peanuts. It was a good decision my father made to plant peanuts. He sold them at a good price to the owner of the threshing machine.

By the end of November, we were picking up pecans. Amon was a natural pecan thresher. He would cut a sapling about twelve feet long, climb a pecan tree and beat the pecans off. They would fall like a hail storm to the burlap blanket Grandma had cut and sewed together. It was spread beneath the pecan tree to catch the pecans.

When no more pecans were left on the tree, the pecans were rolled into a pile and scoped into gunny sacks. We would wait for a windy day, climb a ladder set against the barn and pour out the pecans on a blanket below. The wind would blow the hulls and trash away, leaving clean pecans to be sacked and sold in Henryetta. This cash crop would buy clothes and shoes for the winter. I dreaded the winter, because I would have to wear shoes again.

In the late fall of 1940, my mother's brother, Earl Cooley, moved into a house just over the railroad track from Wilson's store. He had two daughters, Hazel and Lois. My cousins were older than Ed and I. Hazel was fourteen, and Lois was twelve.

My father and uncle Earl worked together plowing under the spent crops. My uncle would farm some land just east of his house the following spring. And because they moved here so late in the year, they were not able to have a garden. So one day my mother boxed up some quart jars of canned green beans and tomatoes, and took them to their house. They were very glad to get the food.

Grandma and Amon would stay through Christmas, and then go back to Muskogee. I had given my mother money I'd saved to order my BB gun, and I was excited. She would not tell me whether or not she had ordered it. She would just say, "I'll see what Santa Claus has to say about it."

Christmas morning finally arrived and Ed and I were up early. My mother and grandma were already busy cooking breakfast and preparing the Christmas dinner. There was no BB gun that I could see.

"Good morning boys," Grandma said. Since you've been good little boys, I have something for you."

She wiped her hands on her apron and went into the bedroom where she and Amon slept. She came out with something long and wrapped in brown paper. "Here, this is for both of you."

We unwrapped the package. I opened the end of the long box, and out slid a brand spankin' new Red Rider BB gun. I yelled, "Grandma! it's what I've always wanted. Thank you."

"It's for both of you. You can take turns shooting it," she said.

My father and mother, being more practical gave us new shoes and clothes to wear. It was a wonderful Christmas, a Christmas that my brother and I had never had before. My father had killed some ducks the day before, so we had duck and all the trimmings for our Christmas dinner. I didn't eat much, because I couldn't wait to try out my, our, new BB gun.

The day after Christmas, Grandma and Amon caught the Motor Coach back to Muskogee, and Ed and I finally had our bedroom back. I missed my Grandma.

The next day Ed and I took our new BB gun behind the tool shed for target practice. As we walked east of the tool shed, we jumped a rabbit out of some weeds and it ran back toward the shed. There were several old rusted oil well pipes along the backside of the shed, and the rabbit ran into one of them. The pipe was six inches in diameter and fifteen feet long.

It was Ed's turn to shoot the BB gun, so I ran to the far end of the pipe to keep the rabbit from running out the other end. I got down on my knees and looked in to the pipe to make sure he was still in there. Just as I looked, Ed shot. The BB hit me in the left eye. I screamed, as blood ran down my face.

When my parents heard me scream, they came running to where we were. "What happened!?" my mother yelled as she came to me.

"I shot at the rabbit in the pipe," Ed said, crying. "I didn't mean to shoot Billy. I didn't know he was looking in the other end of the pipe."

"Give me that damn gun!" my father demanded, as he yanked the gun from Ed's hand.

My mother was wiping the blood from my face with her apron. My eye was throbbing and I couldn't see a thing out of my eye. It scared me to death.

My father walked over to the Cottonwood tree, swung the gun, and wrapped it around the tree. No more BB gun.

"Charlie," my mother said hysterically. "We need to get Billy to the doctor in Henryetta, now!"

My mother held a damp towel over my eye all the way to town.

The doctor examined my eye and said, "The BB hit his pupil and shattered part of it. If we can keep the shattered part from falling down and covering what's left of the main pupil, he may be able to see again."

It was too much for my father. He fainted and fell back against a trash can in the doctor's office. The doctor put something under his nose and he woke up. After that, he was fine.

The doctor bandaged my eye and told my parents that I would need to lie down for a few days. I was not to bend over or strain myself for a couple of days. He wanted to see me again in a week.

I got tired of being still and not doing anything. I had never rested that long in all my life. I peeked under the bandage, but I still couldn't see anything. I was blind in my left eye. I felt sorry for Ed. He was taking it pretty hard. He didn't mean to shoot me. He was just trying to get the rabbit.

A week later, the doctor removed the bandage. I opened my left eye, nothing. I was blind as a bat in that eye. The doctor said the scattered part of the pupil had stayed above the main part of it, and in time, he thought I would get some of my vision back.

Several weeks later, I began to see some light out of my injured eye, then, blurred vision. I could make out images, but they were blurry. It did not get any better. I felt that I would go through life a freak. I had two pupils in my bad eye.

I never knew my grandparents on my mother's side. They died before I was born. Nor did I know my grandfather on my father's side. As I recall, my father only spoke of his father one time.

One day while hunting with our father, we sat down on a log, and he told this story to my brother and I. He said, "My mother, your grandmother, when she was a young woman, she would take in borders to help pay the bills. My father was one of those borders. I never saw my father until I was about your age. He came to the house one day and knocked on our door. My mother opened the door, and caught her breath."

"Hello Minnie," he said.

"Al Spencer!" she cried. And they kissed and hugged each other. She turned and pointed to me and said, "That's Charlie, your son."

"He is a fine boy." He said. "How about you and me go to the river and fish a little today? You want to go?" he asked.

"If mamma will let me," I answered.

"When you come back, I'll have something for you to eat," momma said.

"It was a couple of miles to the Arkansas River," Dad continued his story.

"He had set a trotline out the night before. He said the flat bottom river boat he was using belonged to a friend of his. He got in the front of the boat and I was in the back. He picked up the line and began running it. He took off two channel catfish in the first twenty feet from the bank. We had gone perhaps fifty feet from the bank when the line pulled his hand down into the water."

"Charlie, my boy, I think we've got a big one," he said excitedly.

"For half an hour my father fought that fish, pulling his arm down time after time. Finally a huge flathead catfish was pulled to the surface of the water. The head of the fish was at least fourteen inches across. I could only see part of its body. I had never seen a fish that big before."

"My father had a six inch gaff hook welded to a long shank of iron with a rope tied to the end of it. He hooked it deep under the jaw of the fish. It immediately slapped the water and went down. He quickly tied the rope to the boat and began paddling back to shore. It was not an easy task."

"When we finally reached the bank, I jumped out. My father untied the rope, jumped up on the bank and began pulling on the rope. It was a struggle. Another fisherman who had come to the river in a buggy, pulled by a mule, watched my father struggling to pull the catfish to the bank. He got out of his buggy and ran down to help my father. It took both men to drag the fish out of the water and up the bank. The two men struggled to lift the fish onto the buckboard. Its head and half its body was in the buckboard, the rest of it was hanging off the end with its tail touching the ground."

"I was excited and scared at the same time. I'd never seen anything like this in my life. The man agreed to take us and the fish to weigh it. The man said it was probably a record for a flathead catfish. We arrived at a place that had a cotton scale. It took both men to hoist the fish up and hook it on the scale."

"One hundred and ten pounds," the man said. "That has to be a record. What are you gonna do with it?"

"There are a lot of hungry people in Muskogee. Maybe the Salvation Army could use it. It'll feed a lot of people," my father suggested.

"Well, I've got the buggy, if you'll help me put it back in there, I'll take it down there," the man volunteered.

"It's yours, do with it whatever you want," my father said.

"They put it in the man's buggy and secured it with part of the rope. He unhooked his gaff hook, and my father and I went back to the river, pulled the boat farther up on the bank, and with our two channel catfish started back home."

"My mother had a wonderful meal cooked for us. We ate and talked about the fish and other things way into the night. I was so tired that I fell asleep. When I awoke the next morning my father was gone. I never saw him again. A few years later, my mother told me that she heard that he got in bad with the law and was killed."

After my father told us the story about his father, he stood up and said, "Let's go get a rabbit boy's."

It was an exciting story. I felt sorry for him. He never mentioned his father to us again.

Chapter 9

It seemed that Monday morning came too quickly. I wanted to go back to bed and sleep for days. No school, no chores, no nothing to make life unpleasant. 'We can rest all winter,' Grandma was fond of saying, and it was true, compared to spring and summer. Once the cotton was picked, and the fields plowed under, the pecans harvested, our little farm rested through the cold months. But we still had chores to do, and hunting.

The winter was spent going to school, playing basketball on a frozen dirt court, and coon hunting. We had two coon hounds, Andy, and Skipper. The following year we got a third hound, Rowdy. He was a big dog. He could crush a coon's chest in an instant.

We would go hunting on a Saturday night so we could sleep in on Sunday. We would leave the house with our dogs, a lantern, carbide light, an axe, and head for the river.

When the hounds hit a coon trail, we would listen to determine which direction they were heading. My father enjoyed listening to the hounds. He called it 'Mountain Music'. You knew by the way they barked when they treed a coon. We would run to where the dogs were, flash the light up in the tree to find the coon. My father would climb the tree to flush out the coon, and as soon as it hit the ground the fight was on.

Coons are ferocious fighters. Eventually the dogs would kill the coon, but in the process, they would come away with a lacerated nose, ears split open, and bloody. When the coon was killed, sometimes we would build a fire to get warm and let the dogs rest a bit. Then we would do it all over again. I would be so tired that when we got home near daylight, I would sleep most of the day.

On occasion, Sonny and Wilbur would go opossum hunting with us boys. We would kill the opossum and skin him. Sonny and Wilbur would take the meat, and Ed and I would take the hide. They thought they were getting a good deal, and so did we, so I guess we both got blessed.

We would sell the hides anywhere from ten cents to twenty-five cents a hide. Coon hides would bring more.

One day after school, I decided to take the rifle and go hunting. I took the hounds and headed toward Wolf Creek, and then followed the tree line east along the foot of Tiger Mountain. As we approached the river, the saplings and brush grew quite dense and difficult to get through.

The dogs began barking. I could tell by the way they were barking that it was different than their bark when chasing a rabbit or treeing a squirrel. It was kind of a warning bark. They were up ahead near the river, so I hurried through the brush to see what was going on.

A man was standing beside a large metal container with his gun pointed at my dogs. When he saw me, he swung the gun toward me.

"What you doin' here, boy?"

"Hunting," I said, a little scared.

"This here's my territory. You got no business here," he warned.

I called my dogs to me, and he lowered his gun. "I don't mean no harm Mr. I'll take my dogs and hunt up the river."

He stepped toward me. "What's your name, boy?"

"Billy," what's yours?"

"Ed Groany," he said. "Are you Charlie's boy?"

"Yes sir, one of 'um."

"I know your daddy. I bought some corn from him." He hesitated, then said, "Can you keep a secret?"

"Yes sir. I got a lot of secrets I been a keepin'."

"Good, because nobody needs to know about this here place. You see, this is what we call a "Still," he explained.

"What's that?" I asked.

"You see that stuff behind me?"

"Yes sir."

"Well, that's how we make moonshine. Some folks call it white lightening."

"What's moonshine," I asked.

"Moonshine is rot gut whiskey. This here is a dry State, and it's against the law to make it. So, don't tell nobody, okay? It'll be our secret."

"I can keep a secret. I have some now that I'm a keepin'," I promised.

"Now take your dogs and go on huntin', and don't tell no one."

"Yes sir," I said. I was glad to get away from there. On the way back home, I debated whether or not I should tell my father, but I made a promise, so I decided I wouldn't say anything, at least for now.

The snow started Wednesday afternoon as we ran home from school. It snowed all through the night. When we got up the next morning, I measured the snow at eighteen inches. To an eight year old boy, it came up past my knees.

"Can't we stay home from school," Ed suggested. "Billy and I could go hunting. Them rabbits would be sittin' ducks."

"No, you're going to school," mom stated firmly, as if it had already been determined. "Your father went to the barn to get burlap sacks. He said he'll tie them around your boots to help keep your feet warm."

It was tough going, pushing through that much snow. It was up to my waist in drifts. It seemed that we walked for hours, but it was less than an hour. The last quarter of a mile was the longest. It was all uphill against the north wind. We were frozen when we got to school. We shook off the snow, took the burlap off our boots, and warmed ourselves near the Pot Belly Stove that Mrs. Rose had going. A lot of kids didn't come to school that day, so the teacher told those who were there that school would be dismissed for Friday. That was good news to my frozen ears.

To me, the most disappointing thing about days like this is that I couldn't play basketball at recess. I had gotten quite good at dribbling the ball. I could maneuver around the gofer holes and uneven ground of our dirt court. I dreamed of being a star basketball player when I went to High School.

It was a cold winter, but our cast iron stove kept us warm. And with cured ham in the smoke house, and all the vegetables my mother had canned last summer, we did just fine.

Occasionally, the Williams or Henry's would come down to play pitch with my parents. Clarence and Bertie Henry had two children, Doris and Philip. We played games while the adults talked and played cards. I could tell that Doris liked my brother. I think she had a crush on him.

It was the spring of 1941 and school would soon be out. My father was busy plowing and getting the ground ready for planting corn and cotton. This would be our second year in the river bottom. I looked forward to going barefoot until fall, but not chopping and picking cotton. The Nolan's decided to stay for another year. My father was happy about this, because he needed their help. I was happy because Jessie might need me as a lookout at Wolf Creek this summer.

Saturday afternoon we made a trip to Henryetta. My mother needed flour, sugar, cornmeal, and such. As we drove toward Henryetta, we noticed the sky darkening to the north and west. The night before, according to the radio, heavy rains hit Logan and Lincoln counties several miles northwest of us. Some places received as much as six inches of rain. Logan County was several miles upstream of the Deep Fork River. The creeks and streams were flooding and pouring into the river.

There was no movie, Grapette soda pop, or candy bar this trip. My father was anxious to get what was needed and head home before the rains began.

Lightning flashed, then, a crack of thunder sounded, as we turned off the highway toward Bartlett. It began to sprinkle before we reached Wilson's store at the bottom of the hill. Then more lightning and thunder as the road became slick and muddy.

When we finally pulled up in front of the house, we grabbed the bags of supplies and ran into the house. The rain poured off the roof of the house.

"Well, one good thing about the rain, at least we'll have a full cistern of fresh water," my father said. "And I haven't planted the corn or cotton yet, so if it floods, our crop may be delayed a bit, but we'll still have cotton to chop and pick."

Before I fell asleep that night, I prayed for rain. I asked God to send the biggest flood since Noah, a character in the Bible that Grandma told me about.

The next morning at breakfast the rain had stopped, and my father came into the house. One look in his face satisfied our curiosity. "Rivers at flood stage," he said to us as he took his seat and began reaching for a biscuit and then the gravy. "And there's lightning to the west."

My mother didn't smile or frown, but she had a curious look of contentment. She was determined not to spend her life scratching out a meager existence from this land, and a lost crop could only hasten her departure.

By the time we finished eating, we heard thunder again. Mother cleared the table while listening to the radio to see how rough the storm would be. I thought my prayer was about to be answered, and I felt guilty for such a devious wish.

It rained off and on for two days and the river was out of its banks. Soon it covered the lower half of the cotton field. Each day the flood waters crept through the field and toward our house. The entire river bottom became a huge lake. Wildlife fled toward Tiger Mountain, and I saw a lot of snakes. My father was worried that as much water that fell up river, it might reach our house. It did. The next morning flood waters had risen to a point just below the door of our house.

"What are we gonna do Charlie?" my mother asked, in a concerned voice.

"It's too late to walk out of the bottom. We'll just have to wait it out" he said.

Water never got into our house but came up to the bottom of the floor. We had canned vegetables under the house, but they were sealed, so maybe they'd be alright. When she canned in the summer, the jars were put under the house because it was much cooler there than anywhere else.

It took about ten days for the flood to subside, and another week for the ground to dry out enough for my father to rework the soil and finish planting.

Flooded Cotton Patch

The Flooded Deep Fork River Bottom

Chapter 10

When school was out, I hunted a lot with Boots Conklin. We would get two or three rabbits every time we hunted together. Boots would take the rabbits one time, and I would take them the next. Rabbit was a staple food for our families.

One day Richard and Roy came to our house with Max, Leroy, and a cousin, Kenneth Bonham. They wanted me and my brother to go swimming with them at Wolf Creek. It was always fun to have the Bartlett kids to play with.

It had been some time since the flood, and Wolf Creek was lower than usual. We stripped off our clothes and jumped in. The water was clear, cool, and refreshing. Kenneth walked out on the low water dam and jumped in head first into the water. It was a moment before he came up, but when he did there was blood running down his face. He had hit his head on a rock. We did belly flops after that.

The cotton and corn was a foot high and time to start chopping. For the next several weeks we would be in the field ten hours a day. With the Nolan's helping us, it meant less chopping for me.

I would do my best to keep up with my parents, but not Ed. When we finished chopping a row of cotton, we would have to chop back on his row to get him caught up with us. Chopping cotton was not his favorite thing to do. He was day dreaming of what might be, and singing some Bob Wills song he had heard on the radio. That's what he enjoyed more than anything. I thought he must be destined to be a great singer.

My grandmother on my father's side was half Cherokee Indian. Her ancestors were forcibly removed from their land in the southeastern part of our country. It was known as "The Trail of Tears." They were forced to leave in the middle of winter, and many of them died on their way to Oklahoma.

Minnie Martin, my grandmother, was such a wonderful grandmother to us. She was so funny. She told me that the reason mosquitoes didn't bite me, was because I had Indian blood. My mother didn't believe it.

It seemed that everyone anticipated the World Heavyweight Championship fight between Joe Louis and Billy Conn. The scheduled fight was to be on June 11, 1941 at the Polo grounds in New York City.

The evening of the fight, we all gathered around our battery powered Philco radio to listen to the fight. Louis was nicknamed "The Brown Bomber." As we listened, Conn had the better of the fight through twelve rounds, but Louis was able to stun Conn with a left hook, cutting his eye and nose, and knocked Conn out with two seconds left in the thirteenth round.

It was very exciting to listen to that historic fight. Years later, I would learn that Joe Louis held the Championship of the heavyweight title from 1939 to 1949.

After the flood, it was hot and dry for most of the summer of '41, with only an occasional shower to break the heat. By the middle of August, the cotton was cultivated and laid by. My father wanted to spend a week at the Illinois River near Gore, Oklahoma. He asked Fred Conklin to take care of our home chores, the chickens, hogs, and other live stock while we were gone.

My mother packed up her cast iron skillet, corn meal, flour, bacon grease, coffee, salt and pepper, and a few odds and ends she would need for camping.

When we arrived at a place called "Bills Bluff" on the river, I was in awe of its beauty. The river was two hundred feet wide, with huge Ash, Oak, and Cottonwood trees at least a hundred feet tall, and the water was crystal clear.

After we set up camp, Ed and I wanted to scout out the place.

"You boys don't go off too far, there are wild hogs in this area," Dad said.

We made our way up the river to a bluff that jutted out some one hundred feet above the river. We could see two creeks in the distance that emptied into the river. As we made our way down to the river under the bluff, we noticed areas where wild hogs had rooted up the ground. We cautiously looked around and continued to explore. This had to be the most beautiful place in the world that I'd ever seen.

The area beneath the bluff was an exciting find. About ten feet above the river, rock from the bluff acted as a canopy, leaving an opening that went back about sixty feet.

"Maybe we could camp out here, and our pappy could put his trotlines in the river here," Ed suggested.

We walked up the river a ways to a clear creek that emptied into the river. It was about twenty-five feet wide and very deep. In fact we could see large bass swimming lazily five or six feet under the clear water.

"Billy!" What a place to swim," Ed said excitedly.

"There's nobody around neither. We could swim in our birthday suits," I answered.

"Let's go back and tell pappy about this place," Ed said.

We made our way back up the side of the bluff and toward camp. About half way back to camp we ran into some wild hogs. All of them scattered except one old sow with little ones. She faced us, staring us down. We were in a lot of timber, and as we looked to see which trees we might climb, she charged us.

"Get up that tree by you, Billy!" Ed shouted, as he quickly climbed one near him.

I didn't need to be told twice. We quickly climbed to about ten feet off the ground, and waited. She hung around the base of the trees for half an hour or so. Finally, she lumbered off with her little ones following. We were afraid to get down, so we stayed a while longer before we eased down.

"Let's make a run for it, Billy!" Ed whispered.

We took off. There was nothing that was going to catch us. About half way to camp, I passed Ed. My heart was pounding with fear. I found out that when I'm really scared, I can run faster. I beat him into camp by twenty yards.

We told our parents about the hogs first, and then about the paradise we found up river.

Dad had rented a flat bottom river boat with oars from down river, and paddled up river to our camp. We put our fishing gear in the boat and went up river to just below the bluff and set out a trot line. Before leaving home, we had seined about a gallon of Crawdads for bait and had them in a wet burlap sack with some green grass to keep them alive.

After we baited the trotline, we came back down river to camp. Dad's plan was to run the trotline a couple of times during the night.

All of this was new to me, and my brother and I were very excited. We snacked on food that mother had brought from home, and relaxed for the evening. The stars seemed to be so much brighter here on the river, than at home.

I managed to stay up to go with my father and Ed to run the trotline the first time. Ed held the lantern as we sat in the back of the boat, while pappy worked the oars, making our way up river. The trotline was tied to a willow sapling near the edge of the bank. It was bent down toward the water, and we knew we had fish on the line.

Pappy picked up the line from the front of the boat, and began to pull it up, which had weights to keep the line near the bottom of the river. As he passed the line through his hands, the line suddenly jerked down. He lifted the line up out of the water and flipped a channel catfish into the boat. I judged it to be about three pounds.

"We're eating catfish tomorrow, boys," he said joyfully.

We took off five channel catfish and one flathead, weighing from two to six pounds. We baited the empty hooks and headed back to camp.

Ed went with our father on the three O'clock run. They caught three more fish. I just couldn't stay awake for it. But I was awake for the six O'clock run. My mother said she would have spam and eggs when we returned from running the trotline.

The willow sapling was bent into the water. It would come up out of the water, then down again. "Wow," I said. "We must have a big one."

Dad picked the line up out of the water and moved the line and hooks behind him. We had gone about a third of the way out into the river with no fish, but the line would still pull his hands down into the water.

"Must be hooked on a log," he said.

Suddenly there was a powerful jerk on the line. "No, it's not a log. It must be Ole Dad." It was an expression he had for a big catfish.

He worked the line slowly, bringing the line to the surface of the water. It was daylight enough to see now. He strained, pulling the line up, and suddenly a huge Flathead Catfish appeared near the surface of the water.

"Holy Crap!" my father said. "You boys see Ole Dad?"

The head of the catfish looked to be at least twelve inches wide, and his body, maybe four or five feet long. I immediately thought of the catfish my father told about our grandfather on the Arkansas River when he was a boy.

"Give me the gaff hook," he said, reaching back with one hand while holding the line with the other.

I heard a gurgle, and the huge flathead began backing off the line. Out of his mouth slid a half eaten channel catfish that must have weighed at least five or six pounds, and then he disappeared.

"We've lost him," my father said with a sigh.

He unhooked the half eaten channel catfish, and dropped the line back into the river.

As we made our way back to camp, I was speechless. I had just witnessed the biggest catfish I'd ever seen.

"How much you think he'd weigh?" Ed asked pappy.

"Well, based on what I saw, and the weight of other big catfish I've caught, I'd say somewhere between sixty and seventy pounds."

"Maybe we can catch him again," I stated, as we pulled the boat up on the bank at camp.

"Not likely, son," my father answered. "But we'll catch all we need to eat, and some to give away."

My mother had fried spam and scrambled eggs for us to eat. Ed and I quickly told her all about the big fish that got away.

"He looked to me to be about six feet long and probably weighed near a hundred pounds," Ed said, with excitement. It was a Spencer trait to exaggerate a bit, especially when there were only a few eye witnesses.

What a wonderful week we spent on the most beautiful river I'd ever seen. My father said he'd heard talk about a damn being put somewhere on the river. He said, "If that happens, water would cover everything we now see. It would be nothing but a huge deep lake, and would cover everything but the top of the bluff."

When we returned home the cotton looked like it had grown a foot. Everything else looked the same. Dad asked me to run up to the Conklin's and thank Fred for taking care of things while we were gone. It was good to see Boots again.

We didn't go to Henryetta every Saturday like most folks did. Ed and I played often with the Nolan boys, Sonny and Wilbur. One Sunday afternoon I was shooting hoops with my rolled up burlap sack, hoping desperately that Jessie would happen by on her way to Wolf Creek. Instead it was Wilbur.

"Billy," he said. "I saw a big turtle in the creek by our house. If I had your rubber slingshot, I could kill it."

"I can make you one," I said.

"You can?"

"Sure, my daddy made this one here." I took it out of my back pocket to show him. "I never leave the house without this weapon in my pocket."

There was a willow grove across the creek from which my father had cut my shooter last year. We walked across the old swinging bridge that was built for the oil workers a couple of decades ago. It was a little scary, because it swayed back and forth as you walked across.

We found a limb with a perfect yoke in it. I broke off the limb and carried it back to the house. There was a red rubber tire inner tube in the old tool shed. While my mother was in the garden, I managed to sneak her butcher knife and scissors out of the house. We cut the limbs off to make a perfect yoke, and cut two strips of rubber about a half inch wide and a foot long. We found an old shoe and cut the tongue out of it to make the pouch. We tied it all together and made Wilbur his weapon.

I gave him a couple of smooth round rocks I had in my pocket, and we walked back around the creek to his house. As we approached the foot log that lay across the creek, Wilbur whispered, "Thar he is, you see him?"

He was across the creek near the foot log on a steep bank.

"Shoot him, Wilbur," I whispered.

He shot and missed a foot to the right. When the rock hit the mud, the turtle turned sideways and stuck its head out. I took dead aim and busted him up beside his head. He was stunned, so I quickly ran across the foot log and grabbed him. He was a big snapper. I would guess about ten pounds. My grandmother always told me that if one of them bit you, he wouldn't turn loose until it thundered. I really didn't believe that, but I wasn't about to let him bite me.

Coal Creek in Deep Fork River Bottom

We took it to Wilbur's house. Mammy Nolan was sitting under a shade tree with Jessie and her little sister. There was also a stranger I'd never seen before.

"Mammy Nolan," I said. "Do you want this turtle to eat? Grandma says the meat of a turtle tastes like chicken."

"Oh yes," she said. "I'll try it, and thank you, Billy."

Jessie never even spoke to me. It seemed that she had eyes only for this black stranger.

Wilbur and I left. We decided to walk down the creek to shoot snakes and turtles. As we walked along, I asked Wilbur, "Who was that stranger?"

"He's no stranger," Wilbur said. "He would come to our house in Grayson and see my sister. He came down here to visit us."

"I think he came down here to see Jessie," I said. "What's his name?"

"Rufus. He lived near us in Grayson."

"How long is he gonna stay?" I asked. I had a lot of questions.

"Don't know," he said, as we walked down the creek.

Chapter 11

It was time again for the School Annual Pie Supper. I wasn't interested anymore. Richard would probably win the bid for Charlene's pie again, and of course, he would get to eat it with her. As far as I was concerned, he could have her old pie.

As usual, we enrolled for the School year, and then given a grace period to pick cotton before school would actually start.

It was September, and Amon and Grandma were back with us. My mother said Amon was Grandma's seventh husband. I never asked her about that, I was afraid to. I think my mother exaggerated a bit, as usual. Amon was a tall, skinny man, and a good worker. He was always nice to us boys.

It was cotton pickin' time again. Dad's quota for us boys increased to one hundred and fifty pounds a day. His reasoning was that we were older, so we should be able to pick more cotton. Our birthdays were in August. Ed was now eleven, and I was nine.

The Nolan's met in front of the house early Monday morning. Jessie didn't speak. She seemed to be preoccupied, looking back toward her house in the distance.

My father had the mules already hooked to the wagon. We loaded up and made our way to the east end of the cotton patch. The cotton trailer was already there.

I didn't know why Jessie was acting the way she was, but I suspected it had to do with Rufus.

The evening before, I watched my father patch an inner tube on our old car when Jessie appeared in the distance. It was late but not yet dark, and she seemed to cling to the long shadows as she moved toward the tool shed east of the house. I watched her until she stopped and waved for me to follow. I slipped away toward the tool shed, and within seconds we were walking along a path toward Wolf Creek.

"Where you goin'?" I finally ask, after it became apparent she was not going to speak first.

"I don't know. Just walkin'."

"You goin' to the creek?"

She laughed softly, and said, "You'd like that, wouldn't you, Billy? You want to see me again, don't you?"

My cheeks burned, and I couldn't think of anything to say.

"Maybe later," she said.

Jessie was always mysterious, always moody, and I adored her completely. Walking with her along the narrow path made me feel twenty years old.

"My father's worried about ya'll leavin'," I said.

"My parents ain't leavin', Billy. They need the money."

We stopped walking. She was looking at me, and I was staring at my feet. She tried to say something, but couldn't, then turned and started back toward the house. I tagged along, certain that she was trying to tell me something. She said good night and disappeared into the darkness. Later I would understand what she was trying to tell me.

I hated picking cotton, but I knew I could pick the quota my father had placed upon me. My grandmother had bragged on my cotton picking. She said I was a natural, whatever that meant. So to please her, and show my father I could even exceed my quota of one hundred and fifty pounds, I picked a row, slung my cotton strap over my shoulder and started down a row, as if I could do the whole patch in one day. I went after that cotton like a biting Sow. (An expression I heard my grandmother say)

By mid afternoon, I was nearing the end of a long row of cotton close to the timber that bordered Coal Creek, when I heard voices. The stalks were especially tall, and I was lost in the midst of the foliage. The sun was hot, and sweat dripped from my nose and chin. I had planned to make the turn and then head back to the trailer, working hard and looking forward to the end of the day.

When I heard people talking, I sat on my cotton sack without making a sound. I couldn't tell how far away they were. For a long time I heard nothing at all, the voice of the girl barely made it through the stalks to where I was hiding. She was somewhere to my right several rows away.

I slowly stood and peeked through the cotton but saw nothing. Then, with my cotton sack abandoned, I silently crawled through the stalks, stopping every couple of rows to listen, until I heard her again. She was several rows over, hiding I thought, in the cotton. And then I heard her laugh. A laugh that was soft and muffled by the cotton, and I knew it was Jessie.

I waited on all fours and tried to imagine what she was doing hiding in the field near the creek, as far away from the cotton trailer as possible. Then I heard another voice, that of a man. I decided to move a little closer.

I slithered through a few rows without making a sound. There was no wind to rustle the leaves or bolls of cotton, so I had to be perfectly quiet.

They were quiet for, what seemed to me, a long time. Then there was giggling, both voices at once, low, hushed conversation that I could barely hear. I looked through the stalks and surveyed the situation from ground level. There were no boles or leaves here. I could see something several rows away on the ground. Could it be Jessie's dark hair? I decided I was close enough.

There was no one nearby. The others were working their way back to the trailer. Nothing visible but their straw hats.

Though I was shaded by the cotton, I was sweating profusely. My heart was racing, my mouth dry. Jessie was hiding deep in the cotton with a man, and I thought I knew who he was. They must be doing something bad, or if not, then why was she hiding lying on the ground. I wanted to do something to stop them, but I was just a little kid, a spy who was trespassing on their business. I wanted to leave, but their voices held me.

The snake was a Copperhead, one of many in the river bottom. Like the one my father snapped its head off last year. Each spring it was common to see them chopped up behind our disk and plows. They were medium length, copper in color, thick, aggressive and filled with venom.

If you saw one, you killed it with a hoe or anything you could grab. They weren't as quick as Blue Racers, but they were mean and nasty.

This one was slithering down the row toward me, less than eight feet away. I'd been so occupied with Jessie and whatever she was doing that I'd forgotten everything else. I yelled something, in horror and bolted upright and ran through a couple of cotton rows, stumbled and fell.

A man said something in a loud voice, but for the moment I was more concerned about the snake. I hit the ground and heard someone rushing through the stalks. He was upon me before I could move, his knee in my chest, the switchblade an inch from my nose. We were both breathing hard and sweating profusely, and his odor hit me. Apparently he seldom bathed and took on his own peculiar odor.

"You spying on us, you little shit?" he said, brandishing a long bladed knife near my face.

I shook my head no. Sweat poured from his chin dripped into my eyes and burned. He waved the blade a little, as if I couldn't see it already. I was scared to death.

"You ain't telling anybody what you seen, are you boy?" he warned.

I shook my head no; I couldn't speak. Then I realized my whole body was shaking, trembling in fear. When it was apparent I couldn't utter a word, he took the tip of the blade and tapped my forehead. I think I peed in my pants.

"You speak one word about me and Jessie to anyone," he said slowly, his eyes doing more talking than his mouth, "and I will kill your mother. Understand?"

"Yes sir," I managed, hoping the snake would bite him, but it was long gone when Rufus crashed through the cotton toward me.

"It'll be our little secret." Can you keep a secret? he asked.

"Yes sir," I said. "I'm a keepin' a few now."

"Now get your sack of cotton there and beat it."

I got up, put the strap over my shoulder, and dragged my cotton sack back toward the trailer, escaping like a thief in the night. I had peed in my pants, but no one would notice, I thought, because they were soaked with sweat. When I reached the cotton trailer, I was shaking and felt sick to my stomach. My mother thought I had a heat stroke.

"Charlie, I'm taking Billy to the house. He's had too much sun." momma stated.

I was sick, but I must admit, I faked it a bit, with tears and my hands holding my stomach.

When we reached the house, I took off my overalls and washed up a bit. I put some clean clothes on and laid down with my mother fussing over me. "Your granny will know what to do when she gets here."

Oh no, I thought, Grandma was happiest when she was playing doctor, and I knew I would get the full treatment. When she came to where I was laying, I acted like I was asleep.

A loud thunderstorm hit just as we were sitting down for supper. The sound was a great relief for me. Maybe we wouldn't be going to the field tomorrow.

They watched as I picked at my food. "I'm okay," I said at one point.

The rain fell heavy and loud onto our tin roof, drowning out our conversation so that we ate in silence, the men worrying about the cotton, the women worrying about me.

I had enough worries to crush us all.

"Could I finish later?" I asked, slightly shoving my plate away. "I'm really sleepy."

My mother decided that I would go back to bed and rest as long as I needed to.

I wanted to sleep, but when I closed my eyes, I saw Rufus and the switchblade at my face. For a while I listened to the rain, with the men in the kitchen not far away, drinking coffee, I felt safe, and went to sleep.

Sometime during the night the storm passed, but the next morning, before I was up, Grandma came in to check my temperature.

"You got a fever?" she asked, as she placed her hand on my forehead.

If I didn't have a fever yesterday, why would I have a fever this morning?

"I'll stay close by this morning just in case you need me", she said.

I remember the time she fixed a sure fire remedy for my father who had stomach cramps. She had him drink a pint of hot pepper juice. He spent two days in the outhouse, unable to farm, begging for water, which I hauled back and forth in a quart milk jug. I thought she'd killed him. When he emerged—pale, gaunt, somewhat thinner—he walked with a purpose to the house, angrier than I'd ever seen him.

Grandma had a lot of old Indian medical remedies. Over breakfast I'd heard her tell my mother that she'd decided the proper remedy for me would be a strong dose of Caster Oil, a spoon full of sugar with a few drops of kerosene, and some kind of herb she would get at the creek.

I had stopped eating when I heard this. It was her old standby, one she'd used on Ed before when he was sick. It was more powerful than surgery. His ailment was instantly cured as the dosage burned from his tongue to his toes and kept burning. He warned me about Doctor Grandma.

As bad as I hated going back to the cotton patch, I determined rather quickly that it was far better than taking Grandma's medicine.

We were up before sunrise, did the chores, and were seated around the breakfast table. I noticed grandma eye-balling me, so I quickly said, "You know, I've never felt better in all my life. It's amazing what a little rest will do for you."

"I'm so glad son," momma said. "You do look a lot better this morning. But if you feel sick in the cotton patch, you come immediately back to the house."

I thought to myself, that's an inviting prospect, but then again, staying in the cotton patch verses Grandma's Indian remedies was a no brainer.

"On second thought," my mother said. "It may be too soon for you to be in the hot sun. I want you to stay at the house with me today. Tomorrow you'll feel much better."

After the rest of them went to the field, my mother stayed with me around the house. The very thought of telling what I experienced made me weak. We gathered vegetables from the garden. I followed her with a bushel basket, my eyes cutting in all directions, ready for Rufus to leap from nowhere and slaughter both of us. I could smell him, feel him, hear him. I could see his nasty eyes watching every move we made. The weight of his switchblade on my forehead grew heavier.

I thought of nothing but him, and I stayed close to my mother.

"What's the matter, Billy?" she asked more than once.

I was aware that I wasn't talking, but I couldn't force words out. I just wanted a place to hide.

"Nothin'," I said.

"You still tired?

"Yes ma'am."

And I'd be tired for a month if it kept me out of the cotton patch and away from Rufus.

We went back to the house and I helped her clean the vegetables.

"Are you still tired?" she asked.

"Yes ma'am," I said. "I think I'll go lie down."

"You do that," she said. "You'll feel better tomorrow."

When we walked out of the house the next morning, the Nolan family was waiting for us, all of them except Jessie.

"Challee," Jim said. "We have one less picker today. Sometime during the night Jessie ran away with Rufus. We have no idea where they went. They could a caught the Motor Coach at Bartlett, so no tellin' where they went."

"Well, Jim," my father replied. "I'm real sorry about that. I know how you and Mammy Nolan must feel right now. If you don't feel like pickin' today, I understand."

"Thanks Challee," Jim said. "We'll pick. My wife needs somethin' to do to keep her mind off a Jessie."

My heart sank as I thought of her and Rufus in the cotton patch, hiding and doing whatever they wanted to do. Jessie was probably sneaking around now, doing bad things. What if she now used Rufus as her lookout while she bathed in some creek? I couldn't stand the thought.

I dove into the cotton patch with a vengeance. An hour before it was time to quit, I had picked a little over two hundred pounds. I was mad about being on the losing end of things. First, to Richard Williams and Charlene's pie, and now Jessie, who ran away without saying a word to me about it.

That evening after supper, I took Skipper and we walked to Wolf Creek, and there in the woods I yelled all the bad words that I had heard the boys at Bartlett say. I was so disappointed in Jessie. I managed to hate her for what she had done. And when I spewed forth all the foul language I could remember, I dropped to my knees and asked God to forgive me. And I asked God to protect Jessie.

Part Three

The Way We Were

THROUGH IT ALL

Chapter 12

The heat broke in the last part of September. The nights became cool, and the early mornings were chilly. The stifling humidity was gone, and the sun lost its glare. By midday it was hot again, but not August-hot, and by dark the air was light. We waited, but the heat did not return. The seasons were changing, the days grew shorter.

Since the sun didn't sap our strength as much, we worked harder and picked more. And, of course, the change in the weather was all my father needed to embrace yet another level of concern. With winter just around the corner, he now remembered tales told by men at the cotton gin of staring at rows and rows of muddy, rotting, and unpicked cotton on Christmas Day.

After weeks in the field, I missed school. Classes were about to resume, and I began thinking how nice it would be to sit at a desk all day, surrounded by friends instead of cotton. Hidden inside a cigar box under my bed was the grand sum of $17.50, the result of hard work and frugal spending and investing wisely in the occasional Saturday movie and soda pop, but for the most part my wages were being tucked safely away.

I wanted to order a basketball from Sears, Roebuck, but my mother insisted I wait until the harvest was over. Shipping took two weeks, and I was determined to return to class with my new basketball.

The night was cool and clear, and this prompted my father to predict that tomorrow would be a fine opportunity to pick cotton for twelve hours. Ed and I went to bed dreading tomorrow. I lay awake for some time thinking about Rufus and Jessie, before falling asleep.

At breakfast the next morning, my father was listening to the weather forecast on the radio. It would be cooler than normal, clear, not a cloud in the sky. However, they were having a gully washer in eastern New Mexico, and might be headed our way.

Much of our cotton was still in the field, and my father was anxious to get as much of it picked while the weather cooperated. My mother and grandma finished the dishes in record time, while we finished the outside chores.

I was exhausted by sunrise, and a brief nap crossed my mind, but I knew my father would whip me if he caught me napping.

Lunch was cold biscuits and ham, eaten hurriedly in the shade of the cotton trailer. After about twenty minutes for lunch, my father declared the break was over.

I don't know how much cotton I picked that day, but I'm sure it had to be a world record for a nine year old. When the sun fell behind the trees along the creek, my mother found me and we walked to the house. Ed stayed behind with Sonny trying to pick as much as the adults.

"How long are they gonna work?" I asked my mother.

"Till dark, I guess."

When we got home, I wanted to collapse on my pallet and sleep for a week. But my mother asked me to wash up and help with supper. She made cornbread and warmed up leftovers while I peeled cucumbers and sliced tomatoes. We listened to the radio about a storm in the panhandle of Texas.

In spite of a brutal day in the field, my father and Amon were in good spirits when we sat down to eat. Between them they had picked eleven hundred and forty pounds. If we could just get a few more days of dry weather, then we might survive another year.

The next morning at breakfast I heard a faint rumble of thunder far away, and wondered if anyone else heard it, too. A half hour later the rumbling was much closer, and when lightning flashed and a few seconds later thunder cracked in the distance, it got our attention. The weather report said they were having a Toad Strangler in Oklahoma City.

Soon the winds picked up and the rain began pecking the tin roof, a little too loudly, and grandma said, "It's hail."

We sat at the table for a long time listening to the thunder and rain, wondering how many inches of rain would fall and how long it would be before we could pick cotton again.

The storm passed, but the rain continued. We finally left the kitchen and walked to the front porch. There was nothing but water between the house and the road. I felt sorry for my father as he stood gazing in disbelief at all the water God was sending us.

The next day my parents announced that they were going to town. Outside normal chores, there was nothing to do around the farm. Water was standing between the rows of cotton. Our old Model-A-Ford slowly made its way out of the muddy river bottom. We passed Wilson's store and made a run up the slick clay hill of Bartlett. As we zipped past the Williams place, Gladys was out front looking at her flowers. She waved, and we waved back, and I could almost hear her say, 'Reckon why the Spencer's are headed for town?' We bounced around, slipping and sliding, but finally made it to the top of the hill.

"School starts again on Monday," my mother said, as we passed the school house.

Main Street was quiet. We parked in front of the Barber Shop. A couple of doors down at the hardware store, a group of farmers in overalls were engaged in serious conversation. My father felt obliged to report there first, or at least to listen to their thoughts and opinions on what effect the rain might have on their crops.

My brother and I followed my mother to the drug store where they sold ice cream at the soda fountain. There we received a generous helping of vanilla ice cream covered with cherries. It cost my mother a nickel apiece. We perched ourselves on a stool. We were to stay there for the next thirty minutes while our mother left to buy a few things. We ate slowly, determined to make the ice cream last as long as possible.

People would come in the store and use their telephone. Since most folks didn't have a phone, they'd have to borrow one. Most of the businesses had phones, but we didn't. My mother said that it would be years before they strung phone lines to our place. My father didn't want one anyway. He said that if you had a phone then you had to talk to folks whenever it was convenient for them, not you.

Central Drug Store, Henryetta, Oklahoma.

When we were on our way to town, I heard my mother whisper to my father, something about a phone call. So when we finished our ice cream we went to the grocery store, where we hoped to learn more about the phone call. Our mother was not in the store. Perhaps she wanted a more private phone call without someone listening, I thought. Pearl was at the register, her reading glasses on the tip of her nose, her gaze meeting us the second Ed and I walked in. It was said that she knew the sound of each car or truck that passed along Main Street and that she could not only identify the farmer driving it, but also could tell how long it had been since he'd been to town. She missed nothing.

"Where's your parents?" she asked after we'd exchanged pleasantries.

"We thought they were here," Ed said, looking at the jar of hard candy.

She pointed and said, "have one."

"Thanks," we both said.

"Just you boys and your parents, huh?"

"Yes ma'am. You seen'um?" I asked.

"No, not yet. Are they doing some shopping?"

"Yes ma'am. And I think they need to borrow a phone." This stopped her cold as she thought of all the reasons why my parents needed to call someone. I unwrapped the candy.

"Who they calling?" she asked.

"Don't know." Pity the poor soul who borrowed Pearl's phone and wanted to keep the details private. She'd know more than the person on the other end.

"Y'all wet down there?"

"Yes ma'am, pretty wet." We thanked her for the candy and left the store. The sidewalk was about empty. It was nice to have the town all to ourselves. On Saturday you could hardly walk for all the people. We caught a glimpse of my parents in the hardware store buying something, so we went in to investigate.

On the way home, my mother said she talked to her sister Elsie in California. Aunt Elsie didn't have a phone, so she gave my mother her neighbor's phone number. That's how they were able to talk to each other. "You boys remember your cousins, don't you?"

"Yes ma'am," Ed said. "I remember playing with Slayton. He was two years older than me. I think Dean was about my age, and Delpha was Billy's age."

"Maybe we'll get to see them before long," momma said. "Elsie wants to come back to Oklahoma."

My father had both hands on the steering wheel as we made our way down Bartlett hill. It was slick as snot with deep ruts, but we made it without going into a ditch. We went over the railroad track and down the muddy road to our farm.

When we got home my mother asked me to help her pick vegetables then cleaned them in a washtub outside the back porch. When my mother brought the last basket of greens to the house, she was tired and sweating, and she began cleaning herself with a rag and bucket of water. She couldn't stand to be dirty, a trait she had been trying to pass along to her boys. It struck me as the perfect time for our important conversation. Since Jessie and Rufus were no longer around, I should no longer have to keep this secret.

"Momma, there's something I need to tell you."

"What is it?" she said, wiping her hands on her apron and looking at me as if she'd already decided I'd done something terrible.

There were so many secrets, Jessie at the creek, Ed Groany and his white lightning, Jamie and her hateful words. I had been adept at keeping them private. The current one, though, had to be shared with my mother.

"I think Jessie and Rufus did somethin' bad yesterday."

"Is that so?" she said with a smile, as if I didn't know much because I was just a kid.

"Yes ma'am."

"And what makes you think this?"

"I caught them in the cotton patch the other day."

"What were they doing?" she asked, seeming a little afraid that maybe I'd seen something I shouldn't have.

"I don't know, but they were together."

"Did you see them?"

I told her the story, beginning with the voices, then the snake, then Rufus and my escape. I omitted no details, and, amazingly, I did not exaggerate anything. Maybe the size of the snake, but for the most part I clung to the truth.

She absorbed it and seemed genuinely astonished.

"What were they doing mom?" I asked.

"I don't know. You didn't see anything, did you?"

"No ma'am. Do you think they were kissin'?"

"Probably," she said quickly. I'll talk to your father about it."

I couldn't tell if I felt better about it. She'd told me many times that little boys shouldn't keep secrets from their mothers. But every time I confessed one, she was quick to shrug it off and tell my father what I told her. I'm not sure how I benefited for being candid. But it was all I could do. Now the adults knew about Rufus and Jessie. It might explain why they ran off.

It rained during the night, and the next morning at breakfast I could tell my father was worried about the possibility of losing the crop.

"Jim Nolan told me that his family would help us with the cotton until it was picked," my father said, "but after that, they would be moving back to Grayson."

I hated that they had decided to leave us, but we couldn't expect people to sit around for days, watching the sky, trying to stay dry, and not getting paid. I'm sure they missed their daughter, Jessie too.

Late the next morning, with the sun trying its best to peek through the clouds, they would return to the cotton patch. Ed and I went to school, but when it was over we ran home. Our instructions were to come home after school, change clothes, and pick till dark. We learned that the other pickers did not get into the field until mid-afternoon, because the cotton was too wet and the ground was too soft.

Mud squashed up between my toes, and it stuck to my cotton sack, so after an hour I felt as if I were dragging a tree trunk. We quit before dark and left for the house, a sad and dispirited group of pickers.

I missed Jessie. I tried valiantly to hate her, but it simply wasn't working.

Chapter 13

Each year in late March, my father would begin plowing the fields, turning over the soil, burying the stalks and roots and leaves from the previous crop. He was happy then, pleased to be outdoors after a long hibernation. He would watch the weather and study the almanac, and hear what the farmers were saying, when in town.

He would plant in early May if the weather was right. May 15 was an absolute deadline for putting the cotton seed in the ground. Ed and my contribution began in June, when school would be out and weeds began sprouting. He would give us a sharp hoe, point us in the right direction, and for ten hours a day we chopped cotton, a task almost as hard and mind-numbing as picking the stuff. Most of the summer as the cotton and weeds around it grew, we chopped. If the cotton bloomed by July 4, then it was going to be a bumper crop. By late August or early September we were ready to pick.

But this was October, and all the labor, the sweat and sore muscles, all the money invested in seed, labor, and fuel, all the hopes and plans, everything would be lost if it flooded.

I had never witnessed such silence over supper. The mood was somber. Not even grandma could find anything pleasant to say. I played with my beans and tried to imagine what my parents were thinking. My father was probably worried about the crop loan, a debt that would now be impossible to repay. My mother was working on her escape from the cotton patch. She was not nearly as disappointed as the other three adults. A disastrous harvest, following such a promising spring and summer, gave her the artillery to use against my father for leaving this place.

We could expect some rain in September, but not as much in October, and certainly not a flood. Gladys told my mother that she remembers when the river bottom flooded three times in the same year. This was not an encouraging thought.

The storm from the west woke us up early the next morning. I walked into the kitchen, and my father was at the table, drinking coffee, fiddling with the radio. He was trying to pick up a weather station. Momma was frying bacon.

"We pickin' today daddy?" I asked.

"We'll know directly, his eyes on the radio and sipping coffee."

"Did it rain last night," I asked Grandma.

"All night long, I believe," She said.

Grandma fixed coffee for me and my brother. It was mostly cream and sugar with just a dab of coffee.

As soon as my father took his last bite of eggs, he wiped his mouth, took the last sip of his coffee and looked through the window over the kitchen sink. There was enough light to see what he wanted. "Let's take a look," he said.

The mornings in October became chilly. The seasons were changing; the days grew shorter. The change in the weather was all daddy needed to embrace yet another level of concern. With winter just around the corner, he now remembered tales of staring at rows of muddy, rotting, and unpicked cotton on Christmas Day.

We slipped on a jacket and walked toward the lower end of the cotton field. The river was out of its banks and flood waters were creeping into the lower part of the field. As we started back a breeze came from the west. Before we got back to the house, the wind grew stronger and the sky darker. All of our storms came from the west. Oklahoma was known as Tornado Alley.

Hail hit first, tiny specks like the size of a pea, and we ran for the house. The sky to the west was dark blue, almost black, and the low clouds were bearing down on us. The hail stung the back of my neck and prompted me to run even faster. The wind was howling through the trees that lined the creek and cotton stalks bent to the east. Lightning flashed, and then a loud clap of thunder followed.

The rain hit with a fury. It was cold and sharp falling sideways in the fierce wind. We were instantly soaked. I wouldn't have been better off if I'd jumped in the creek. The rain beat us in waves. It was so blinding I could barely see in front of me. Lightning flashed again and thunder boomed again, this time much closer, so close that my ears hurt. I thought we were going to die.

It seemed that it took forever to get to the house, but when we did, the rain suddenly stopped. The wind ceased. It became deathly still. The sky was even darker, black in every direction. "It's a tornado!" Pappy shouted as we reached the house. To the west, high above the tree line, a slim funnel cloud dipped downward. It was light grey against the black sky, but still some distance away. Tornados were a way of life in Oklahoma, but I'd never seen one until now.

"Rhoda!" my father yelled as we entered the house. He didn't want my mother to miss such a spectacle.

We watched the funnel from the front porch because it was not near our farm, and was going away, to the north. It moved slowly, as if it were searching for the perfect place to touch down. Its tail was clearly visible above the horizon. The funnel spun tightly, a perfect upside-down cone whirling in a fierce spiral.

The twister sank lower and stopped skipping. It appeared as if it had indeed touched down somewhere a few miles away, because we could no longer see the end of it. The cotton gin, the movie theater, Dewar High School—I was tallying the damage when suddenly the twister lifted itself up and seemed to disappear completely. Then it started raining once more, and we went into the house.

The storm raged for a couple of more hours and threw almost everything in nature's arsenal at us: gale-force winds, hail, blinding rain, twisters, and lightning and thunder, so loud that Ed and I hid under the bed at times.

I wasn't sure how we would die—blown away by a tornado or burned alive by lightning or swept away by the water, but it was obvious to me that the end had come.

When the wind and rain finally passed, we went out to survey the destruction. Other than wet cotton and water everywhere, there was surprisingly little damage—several scattered tree branches, some ripped up vegetable plants in the garden, the door blown off the well house. Maybe a week or so of dry weather, and the river is back in its banks, just maybe we'll be back in business.

During a late lunch my father said, "I reckon I better go check on the gin." We were anxious to see what damage had been done. What if it had been leveled by the twister?

"Let' go," Pappy said, and we jumped from our chairs. The dishes were piled in the sink and left unwashed, something I'd never seen before.

Our road was nothing but mud and in large sections had been washed away. We slipped and slid for half of a mile until we came to a crater. Pappy rammed it in low and plowed through the ditch on the left side. My mother was in the front seat with Pappy, Ed and I sat on the laps of Amon and Grandma in the back. Grandma said something to the effect that perhaps it wasn't such a good idea to go to town after all.

We finally made it over the railroad tracks, and managed to stay in the ruts going up Bartlett hill. It was scary, but we made it to the highway. When we turned toward Henryetta, we left a long trail of mud on the asphalt. Why couldn't all roads be paved? I asked myself.

Things appeared normal as we drove along. There were no trees down. Nothing seemed out of place as we moved through Dewar.

When we arrived at Henryetta, the gin was roaring as usual. The stores along Main Street were intact. We weren't the only curious ones. Traffic was heavy on Main Street, and people crowded the sidewalks. This was unheard of for a week day. We parked and scampered to the drug store, where the foot traffic appeared to be particularly thick. Mr. Sims had a group going, and we got there just in time.

According to Mr. Sims, who lived in Schulter, north of Henryetta, he had known a twister was about to appear because his old hound was hiding under the kitchen table, a most ominous sign. Taking his cue from his dog, Mr. Sims began studying the sky, and before long was not surprised to see it turn black. He heard the twister before he saw it. It dipped down from nowhere, came straight for his farm, and stayed on the ground long enough to flatten two chicken coops and peel the roof off his house. A piece of glass struck his wife and drew blood, so we had a bona-fide casualty. Behind me I heard folks whisper excitedly about driving out to the Sims' place to inspect the destruction.

"What'd it look like?" somebody asked.

"Black as coal," Mr. Sims said. "Sounded like a freight train."

This was even more exciting because our twister had been light gray in color, almost white. His had been black. Apparently all manner of tornadoes had ravaged our county.

Mrs. Sims appeared at his side, her arm heavily bandaged and in a sling, and I couldn't help but stare. She looked as though she might pass out on the sidewalk. She displayed her wound and received plenty of attention until Mr. Sims realized he'd lost the audience, so he stepped forward and resumed his narrative. He said his tornado left the ground and began hopping about. He jumped in his truck and tried to follow it. He gave it a good chase through a driving hail storm and almost caught up with it as it circled back.

Mr. Sims truck was older than our car. Some in the crowd began looking around in disbelief. I wanted one of the adults to ask, "What were you gonna do if you caught it." Anyway, he said he soon gave up the chase and returned home to see about his wife. When he had seen it last, his tornado was headed toward Morris.

Pappy told me later that Mr. Sims would tell a lie when the truth sounded better.

There was a lot of lying that afternoon in Henryetta, or perhaps a lot of exaggeration. Twisters were told and retold from one end of Main Street to the other. Pappy described what we had seen, and for the most part he stuck to the facts. The double twister story carried the moment and had everyone's attention until Mr. Sims stepped forward and claimed to have seen three! His wife verified it, and Pappy went to the car.

By the time we left town, it was a miracle that hundreds hadn't been killed.

The last of the clouds were gone by dark. We sat on the porch after supper and listened to the radio. The air was clear and light—the first hint of autumn. There was no conversation between us. The storms and cool weather had struck us like an illness. The seasons were changing, yet nearly one third of the cotton was still out there. Surely it was time for a change.

If the weather was dry and the flood waters receded, it would still be a couple of weeks before the east end of the field could be picked. "It's possible," Pappy said, "that within a week we could start picking here near the house. The ground is higher on this west end."

At least there was some hope.

We had just finished breakfast when there was a knock on our front door. It was Jim Nolan. "Good mornin'," he said. "Ya'll weather the storm yesterday?"

"Yes," Pappy answered. "How did you folks do?"

"Challee," Jim said. "The wind blew so hard it made the old house lean to the east some, and it has stayed that way. It scared us to death. Mammy says we need to go back to Grayson. And so, I'm askin' you a favor. Would you be willin' to take us to Grayson. I know I said I'd stay till the cotton's picked, but it's gonna be wet for some time, even if we have good weather. Besides, we're worried about Jessie."

"I understand Jim," my father said. "Of course I'll take you to Grayson. When do you want to leave?"

"We don't have much to pack. If you think we can get out of the bottom with all the water and mud, we can be ready this morning."

"I'll be over to get your family in about an hour. Is that okay?"

"You is a good man Challee. We'll be ready."

Ed and I rode with our father to pick up the Nolan's. There wouldn't be room for us to ride with them to Grayson, so we would say our goodbyes and walk back home.

The car was hopelessly overloaded. Burlap sacks clung to the sides, loosely secured with baling wire. When they were all loaded and apparently about to leave, Ed and I walked over to say our farewells. They apologized again for leaving before the cotton was picked, but we all knew there was a good chance the crop was finished anyway. They tried to smile and be gracious, but their pain was obvious. We said goodbye to Sonny and Wilbur, and watched them drive away. The Nolan's were off, pots and pans rattling, Sonny and Wilbur sitting on their older sisters laps, crammed in like sardines. We waved goodbye until they were out of sight.

I missed Jessie. I knew now what she was trying to tell me when we had our last walk together. She knew she was leaving, and it was hard to tell me goodbye. I tried to hate her, but it wasn't working. I prayed that God would protect her.

Sunday was gray and overcast. Long after breakfast we sat around the breakfast table, sipping coffee, listening to the radio, worrying about the dramatic change in the weather. My parents were worrying, I was only pretending.

The farm was quiet, no Nolan's, no more thunder, and no more rain. Grandma and Amon had gone back to Muskogee. We were alone again, just us Spencer's, left to battle the elements and try to stay above water. My father had poured his guts into the soil for six months, and now he had nothing to show for it. It seemed to be a losing battle.

"I guess we're done pickin'," I said.

"Sure looks like it," my father said, a little sad as he got up and walked out of the house.

"Why does our land flood so quick?" I asked my mother.

"Because it's lower and close to the river," she said. "That's why I want to leave here. There's not much of a future."

We walked out to the front porch. Ed and I sat on the edge of the porch, our bare feet dangling, swinging back and forth. The sun was behind a cloud, and a breeze shifted into our faces. The trees along the edge of the creek were changing colors to yellow and crimson, and leaves were falling.

"When we move from here, it'll be a new life, one that's far better than this," she nodded toward the field, toward the ruined cotton out there drowning.

Ed left the porch and headed for the back yard, so I thought this would be a good time to unload another secret that I'd been keeping, the one about being a lookout for Jessie.

I began the story, laying sufficient blame on Jessie for everything that might get me in trouble. She'd planned it. She begged me to go with her. She dared me. She'd done this and that. Once my mother realized where the story was leading, her eyes began to dance, and she said every so often, "Billy, you didn't!"

I had her. I embellished here and there, to help move the story and build suspense, but for the most part I stuck to the facts. She was hooked.

"You watched Jessie bathing?" she asked in disbelief.

"Yes ma'am."

"Why did you do that?"

"Jessie made me do it."

"Don't blame Jessie."

"I wouldn't have done it without her."

"Billy, I can't believe you did that." She wanted to scold me, but she was too caught up in the story. She grinned and shook her head in amazement.

"How often did y'all go roaming around like that?"

"I think that was it."

"You liked Jessie, didn't you?"

"Yes ma'am. She was my friend."

"I hope she is happy."

"Me too. Momma, do you think we'll ever see her again?"

"No, I don't think so."

Within a week, we were picking cotton on the west end. Normally, the cotton was picked twice, the second time to clean up what pickers left in the boles. We picked cotton that fall, trying to get as much out as possible.

Food was important for a long winter, one that would follow a bad crop, one in which everything we ate would come from the garden. There was nothing unusual about this, except there wouldn't be a spare dime to buy anything but flour, sugar, and coffee. A good crop meant there was a little tucked away under a mattress, a few dollars rolled up and saved and sometimes used for luxuries like soda pop, ice cream, or white bread. A bad crop meant that if we didn't grow it, we didn't eat.

In the fall we gathered mustard greens, turnips, black-eyed peas, and late producing vegetables that had been planted in May or June. There were a few tomatoes, but they were puny.

The garden changed with the seasons, except for winter, when it was finally at rest, replenishing itself for the months to come.

"Ed, you and Billy, go help your mother in the garden," my father said.

"I'd rather go hunting," Ed said.

"Don't make me repeat myself," he said sternly.

Mom was in the garden waiting for us.

"We have to hurry, much more rain and the greens will rot. And what if the flood water reaches the garden?"

"We wanted to go hunting," Ed said.

"Maybe tomorrow, right now we have to get the turnips out of the ground." Her dress was pulled up past her knees and tied in a knot. She was barefoot with mud up to her ankles. I'd never seen my mother so dirty. We attacked the turnips, and within minutes we were covered in mud from head to foot.

We pulled and picked vegetables for what seemed like hours, then cleaned them in a washtub outside the back porch. When my mother brought the last basket of greens to the house, she was tired and sweating, and she began cleaning herself with a rag and a bucket of water. She couldn't stand to be dirty, a trait she had been trying to pass along to her boys.

It was December the 7th, and while we were eating, there was a news flash on the radio. "We are at war!" the newsman said. "The Japanese just bombed Pearl Harbor!" We sat glued to the radio as the news broke. It said that dozens of ships were bombed or torpedoed and were sinking. There could be thousands of people dead. The news was shocking. Then our President, Franklin Roosevelt, spoke to the people by way of radio.

My father bought a newspaper in town a couple of days later. One article said that in many factories and businesses across America, people were falling on their knees, praying, "God save America." "God protect our boys who fight for freedom."

I was afraid that my father would be leaving to fight the Japanese, but he discovered that he would be exempt from the draft, because America needed farmers on the home front. It was a relief to know my father would not have to fight in some far off war.

A week after Pearl Harbor, Luke Conklin joined the Army Air Force, and within a year or so, made the rank of Major and was leading bombing missions. Fred stayed home to tend the farm and help his mother. We went to see them quite often.

Chapter 14

The spring of 1942 was no different than the others. We were plowing, cultivating, and planting corn, cotton, and vegetables.

If it were not for our two milk cows, hogs, chickens, and garden, I don't think we could have made it. We sold some butter, eggs, and vegetables to a couple of mom and pop stores in Henryetta; ruined vegetables were fed to the hogs.

When my mother washed clothes, she would build a fire under a big black kettle. She scrubbed our clothes with soap on a washboard, and then put them into the kettle of boiling water. She used a part of a broom handle to take them out and put them in a tub of rinsing water. Ed and I would get on each end of a pair of overalls and twist in opposite direction to squeeze the water out. Then she would hang them on the clothes line to dry.

Emmitt Dodge came to our house and asked my father if my brother and I would like to work for him. This was before we started chopping cotton. It would only be for a week. He was baling hay, and needed some help getting the bales out of the field and into his barn. He would pay us a dollar a day. We agreed to do it.

It was hard work. Some bales weighed as much as we did. We would buck the bales up on a trailer, and then take them to the barn to be unloaded and stacked inside.

The afternoons were hot. Sweat soaked our clothes. About midway through the week, Ed got too hot. Emmett took him to some shade and doused him with water and cooled him off some. He didn't work the rest of the day, but the next day we were at it again. We made seven dollars apiece.

All the news each morning was about the war with Japan and Germany. The Government began to ration some things. Some household items were: flour, sugar, and such. They issued books of stamps for each household. One sugar stamp would get you five pounds of sugar each month. However, they didn't take into account that some folks might trade stamps to get more of a certain item they needed. For example: My mother needed ten pounds of sugar because she was canning vegetables. She knew she had one stamp that would get her five pounds. So she traded a different stamp she didn't need to Gladys for a sugar stamp. Now she had two stamps, but the grocery stores were strict in following the government regulations. She sent her two boys to Wilson's store with a sugar stamp each. I stayed outside until Ed came out with his five pounds of sugar. Then I went in and presented my sugar stamp. Mr. Wilson looked at me and said, "Weren't you just in here?"

"No, I answered. That was my brother."

Mr. Wilson just grinned and looked at Mrs. Wilson, then reached behind the counter and gave me my five pounds of sugar.

We had a credit account at the store, as most people did. I had noticed when my mother picked up a few things at the store, she simply said, "Charge it. Would you please put these items on our account," and signed the ticket.

So after Mr. Wilson gave me my five pounds of sugar, I said to him, "Charge it," and signed the ticket like I was someone special.

I told my mother what happened, and she laughed. I had never seen her laugh so hard before. I never did understand why it was so funny.

By the end of August, I turned ten years old and my brother Ed, twelve. By this time we were seasoned choppers and pickers. We could pick almost four hundred pounds of cotton apiece, each day. Pappy (that's what we called our father) and Amon, would pick over five hundred each, and Grandma was right up there with them. Mom didn't pick that much, because she had chores of a morning after we left for the field, and she quit early too prepare supper for us all.

One Sunday afternoon my mother forced me into the garden, where we gathered enough food for fifty people. We washed the tomatoes, cucumbers, okra, carrots, and greens in a tub of water. She then carefully arranged it all in a cardboard box. Grandma put together two dozen eggs, two pounds of cured ham, a pound of butter, and two pint jars of wild blackberry jam.

The Holt family lived across the Deep Fork River between the bridge and the railroad tracks. A story was told that once Mrs. Holt sold some cream to Gladys Williams. Later, one of the kids said that the reason they sold it was because a mouse had fallen in it. They were very poor people, according to Gladys Williams, who told my mother about them. My mother had met Joan Holt at the Annual Pie Auction. I knew the Holt kids, because the older boys attended Bartlett School part of the time. Except for the older boy, Bruce, who was a bully, I felt sorry for them.

"The Holt family needs a little help," my mother told me. "We're going to take a box of vegetables to them."

When we rolled to a stop, five dirty little faces stared at us. Mrs. Holt emerged from the decrepit porch, wiping her hands on her apron. She managed to smile at my mother. "Hello, Mrs. Spencer," she said in a soft voice. She was barefoot, and her legs were a skinny as twigs.

"Nice to see you Joan," my mother said. We didn't expect to see Mr. Holt. Pride would prevent him from coming forward and accepting food.

I studied the house, a square little box, smaller than ours, and wondered once more how all those people could live in such a tiny place. Our well house was almost as large. The windows were open, and the torn remains of burlap sack curtains hung still. There were no screens to keep the flies and mosquitoes out.

It seemed cruel for anyone to live in such conditions. Then I remembered the little two room shack we lived in when we first arrived in the river bottom.

They had no shoes. Their clothes were old and worn. I felt sorry for them. I lifted the box of vegetables out of the car and set it on the dilapidated porch, while my mother called out its contents, and the Holt kids moved around it, eagerly looking on. Bruce, the older boy, stood to one side with his hands on his hips staring at me. He raised his fist and made a face at me. Why would he do that, especially after giving them food. My mother didn't see it, but I did, and I didn't like it one bit.

Mrs. Holt thanked us, and as we drove away, the Holt kids were crawling all over the box of vegetables as if they hadn't eaten in a week.

A couple of weeks later, my mother thought it was time to take the Holt family more vegetables from our garden. Pappy and Ed piddled in the tool shed, so my mother and I loaded three boxes of vegetables and headed for the river. My mother drove, and I prayed, and somehow we made it safely over the river bridge. Just off the bridge, we turned on a one lane dirt road and rolled to a stop in front of their house.

Mrs. Holt emerged from the house and managed a smile, then helped us haul the food to the dilapidated front porch. The women went into the house and I found a spot under a shade tree next to our car, and I planned to loiter alone, just minding my own business while I waited for my mother.

Three of them suddenly appeared from around the house—three boys, with Bruce who was leading the group. The other two were younger, perhaps eleven and ten, but just as lean and wiry as Bruce. They approached me without saying a word.

"Howdy Bruce," I said, trying to at least be polite.

"What're you doin' here?" he growled. He had a brother on each side, all three lined up against me.

"My mother made me come," I said.

"You ain't got no business here." He was hissing through his teeth, and I wanted to back up. In fact, I wanted to tuck tail and run.

"I'm waitin' for my mother," I said.

"We're gonna whup your ass," Bruce said, and all three of them clenched their fists.

"Why?" I managed to say.

"Just cause we can."

The youngest one looked particularly fierce. He was squinting and twisting his mouth up at the corners, sort of snarling at me, and I figured the first punch would come from him.

"Three on one ain't fair," I said.

"No matter," Bruce said and then, quick as a cat, he punched me in the stomach. A horse could not have kicked me harder, and I went down.

I'd had a few scuffles at school—playground push-and-shove that were broken up before serious blows were landed. Mrs. Grace Rose, the teacher, gave me three licks for trying to fight Kenneth Bonham, and Pappy could not have been prouder. I was no stranger to violence. Pappy loved to fight, and when I hit the ground, I thought of him. Somebody kicked me; I grabbed a foot, and instantly there was a pile of little warriors, all kicking and clawing and cussing in the dirt. I threw a couple of quick punches and grabbed the hair of the midsized one while the other two pounded my back. I was determined to yank his head off when Bruce landed a nasty shot to my nose. I went blind for a second, and they, squealing like wild animals, piled on again.

I heard the women yell from the porch. It's about time! I thought. Mrs. Holt arrived first and began pulling boys from the heap, scolding them loudly as she flung them around. Since I was at the bottom, I got up last. My mother looked at me in horror. My nose was oozing warm blood.

"Billy, are you all right?" she asked, grabbing my shoulders.

My eyes were watery, and I was beginning to ache. I nodded my head yes, no problem.

"Cut me a switch!" Mrs. Holt yelled at Bruce. She was growling and still flinging the two smaller ones around. "Whatta you mean beating up that little boy like that? He ain't done nothin'."

The blood was really flowing now, dripping off my chin and staining my shirt. My mother made me lie down and tilt my head back to stop the bleeding, and while we were doing this, Bruce produced a stick.

"I want you to watch this," Mrs. Holt said in my direction.

"No, Joan," my mother said. "We're leaving."

"No, I want your boy to see this," she said. "Now bend over, Bruce."

"I ain't gonna do it, Ma," Bruce said, obviously scared.

"Bend over, or I'll get your father. I'll teach you some manners. Beatin' up that little boy, a visitor to our place."

"No," Bruce said, and she hit him in the head with the stick. He screamed, and she whacked him across the ear.

She made him bend over and grab his ankles. "You let go and I'll beat you for a week," she threatened him. He was already crying when she started flogging away. Both my mother and I were stunned by her anger and brutality. After eight or ten licks, Bruce started yelping. "Shut up!" she shouted.

Her arms and legs were as thin as the stick, but what she lacked in size she made up for in quickness. Her blows landed like machine-gun fire, fast and crisp, popping like a bullwhip. Ten, twenty shots, and Bruce was bawling. "Please stop it, Ma! I'm sorry!"

The beating went on far past the point of punishment. When her arm was tired, she shoved him to the ground, and Bruce curled into a tight ball and wept. By then the other two were already in tears. She grabbed the middle one by the hair. She called him Bobby and said, "Bend over." Bobby slowly clutched his ankles and somehow withstood the assault that followed.

"Let's go," my mother whispered to me. "You can lie down in the back seat." As we were getting into the car, Mrs. Holt was pulling on the other boy, yanking him by the hair. Bruce and Bobby were lying in the dirt, victims of the battle they'd started. My mother turned the car around, and we drove off.

The dust boiled behind us, and I lost sight of them. As I lay down and tried to get comfortable, I prayed that I would never again set foot on their place. I never wanted to see those people for the rest of my life.

My return home was triumphant. Pappy and Ed, Amon and Grandma, they were all sitting on the front porch when we rolled to a stop less than twenty feet away. As dramatic as I could, I got out of the car and stood, and with great satisfaction watched them react in shock at the sight of me. There I was—beaten, bloodied, dirty, clothes ripped, but still standing.

I slowly walked toward them, and everyone gathered around me. My mother stormed forward and very angrily said, "You're not gonna believe what happened! Three of them Holt boys jumped Billy! Bruce and two others caught him while I was in the house. The little criminals! We're takin' food over, and they pull a stunt like this."

"Three of 'um?" Pappy repeated, his eyes dancing.

"Yes, and they were all bigger than Billy," my mother said, and the legend began to grow. The size of my three attackers would increase as the days and months went by.

Grandma was in my face staring at my nose, which had a small cut on it. "Might be broken," she said, and though I was thrilled to hear it, I was not looking forward to her treatment.

"You didn't run, did you?" Pappy asked. He, too, was moving in closer.

"No sir," I said proudly. I'd still be running if given half a chance.

"He did not," my mother said sternly. "He was kickin' and clawin' just as hard as they were."

Pappy smiled.

"We'll go back tomorrow and finish 'um off," Ed said.

"You'll do no such thing," my mother said.

"Did you land a good punch?" Pappy asked.

"They were all cryin' when I left," I said.

My mother rolled her eyes.

"Say there was three of 'um, huh?" Amon asked.

"Yes sir," I said, nodding.
"Good for you, boy, It'll make you tough."
"Yes sir," I said.
"Let's get cleaned up," my mother said.
"You okay, Billy?" Ed asked.
"Yep," I said, as tough as I could.
They led me away in a victory march.

The Deep Fork River had some deep holes, according to my father, and around the bottom of the bridge piers there were Flathead catfish that weighed sixty pounds or more. They were scavengers that moved only when food was nearby. According to Fred Conklin, he and Luke caught one of the monsters when he was thirteen. It weighed forty-eight pounds.

Our family loved catfish. With red worms and crawdads as bait, my brother and I fished the Deep Fork, and always caught fish. It was not a pretty river, even though its banks were lined with oaks, cottonwood, and willow trees. The water was always muddy. It was nothing like the beautiful Illinois River in eastern Oklahoma.

Drownings were not uncommon, and I'd heard colorful tales of grown men caught in quick sand and being swept under by a huge whirl pool, while entire families watched in horror. I'd never witnessed this myself, and the story varied according to the narrator. My mother said it was all fiction. But the story was told so that kids like us would appreciate the dangers of the river.

The cotton patch was waiting with the promise of back breaking labor. Why couldn't I just fish all day? Set by the river in the shade. Anything but pick cotton. I wasn't going to be a farmer. I didn't need the practice. The cotton patch was just a part of our family life, but my mother always told me that some day that would change.

The week began before dawn on Monday morning. We started on the west end of the field. Not a word was spoken. Before us were six endless days of overwhelming labor and heat, followed by Sunday, which on Monday, seemed as far away as Christmas.

Time stopped when we were picking cotton. The days dragged on, each yielding ever so slowly to the next.

When we had hired people picking, they left cotton in the burrs, and that's why we had to pick it the second time. But the six of us were professionals by now, and we gleaned all of the cotton the first picking.

We were in the middle of breakfast on Saturday morning when my father stomped in from the back porch. "There's lightning in the west."

"Can't do anything about the weather," Grandma said.

By the time we finished eating, we heard thunder. The dishes were cleared, and another pot of coffee was made. We sat at the table listening to the radio, waiting to see how bad the storm would be. But the thunder and lightning moved to the northeast. No rain fell. Before eight O'clock we were in the field picking hard and longing for noon.

Sunday afternoons were often used for visiting. It was usually the Henry's from Dewar, or the William's. We would go there, or they would come to our place. Bertie Henry and Gladys Williams were my mother's best friends, and when they got together, there was a lot of talking and laughter.

On one occasion, the Henry's were visiting us. They had two kids, Doris and Philip who were the same age as Ed and I. The adults were playing a card game in the living room, and the four of us kids were playing on the floor of the same room when suddenly I cut a windy. I tried to hold it back, but I couldn't. It was real loud. I mean, it was a blast. Everyone started laughing, except my parents. My father stood up and walked over to where I was sitting on the floor, grabbed my arm and yanked me up and into the bedroom. He beat me half to death. I thought he would never stop. I tried to keep from screaming and crying, because we had company. But it didn't work. I was so embarrassed. Finally, he stopped and told me to never do that again in front of company. I was too embarrassed to go back in the living room. I waited until they left, and then went to bed.

The Wilson's closed their store in the fall of 1942, and the Gaither's moved into the building. Maud Gather was the sister to Mrs. Wilson. Al and Maud Gaither had his kids, her kids, and their kids. They were: Dean, Bud, Patricia, Tommy, Dale, Kenneth, Jerry, Gerldene, and the twins, Joe Don and Trudi Beth. Bud was Ed's hunting partner and best friend.

The Gaither's invited the entire community to a dance on Saturday night. Even though it was chilly, most of the kids played outside in the road. We played games, like, "Red Rover, Red Rover, let (someone's name) come over." That person would run and try to break through a line of kids holding hands. We had a lot of fun.

Inside the building there was music and dancing. My father played the fiddle and harmonica. I forget who played the guitar. I remember one particular song, "Ole Joe Clark." Grandma stepped upon the platform and started dancing a jig to that music.

With sweat dripping off her chin, she danced for at least half an hour. People were throwing pennies and nickels at her feet, so she kept dancing. Finally my father got tired and stopped playing, and Grandma began gathering up all her loot. As I recall, she always carried her money in a Bull Durum sack tied by a cord around her neck. That was her bank.

Occasionally on Sunday, my father would take his boys to a Field Trial. People would bring their dogs to a designated place. Someone would drag a coon hide for half a mile through timber, and then, put it in a tree. There would be bets to see which dog would get to the tree first, second, or third, and bets also on which dog treed at the supposed coon in the tree.

At one such meeting, my father bought us a hamburger, and as we were eating our hamburger, a little boy stood in front of my father looking up at him eating his burger. The boy was six or seven, with a dirty face and ragged clothes.

"Are you hungry, young man?" My father asked.

"Yes sir, he said.

Come with me to the hamburger stand," my father told the boy.

He bought that little boy two hamburgers. The boy had a grin from ear to ear. My father was a giving, caring person. He was my daddy, and I loved him.

Chapter 15

One Sunday I was sitting on the front porch watching my mother and grandmother shelling black-eyed peas and butter beans. My brother Ed and Bud Gaither had gone hunting. My father had the hood up on our old car tinkering with something. It was a beautiful fall afternoon. I was thinking about going over to see if Boots wanted to go shoot some snakes and turtles down on the creek, when I saw a cloud of dust coming from around the bend of the creek. "Cars coming," I said, and they looked in that direction.

Traffic on our road was rare. We watched it without a word. The car moved slowly. I saw a hint of red, and before too long a shiny two door sedan pulled up in front of the house and parked behind our car.

The three of us was now standing on the porch, too surprised to move.

The driver opened the door and got out. Momma said, "Well, it's Carl Cooley." Carl was the son of Momma's oldest brother, Walter.

We all met in front of the car which was new and undoubtedly the most beautiful car I'd ever seen. Everybody shook hands, hugged, and exchanged greetings. Carl introduced his new wife, a thin little thing who looked younger than Jessie. Her name was Opal. She was from the northeast, and when she spoke her words came through her nose, and within seconds she made my skin crawl.

"Why does she talk like that?" I whispered to my mother as we moved to the porch.

"She's a Yankee," was the simple explanation.

Carl said he was working for an aircraft company in Tulsa that had a Government contract to build airplanes for the war. He was making a dollar an hour, an unbelievable wage by our standards. He said Opal came to Tulsa to visit a relative. They met and had a few dates, and then got married.

"That's some car," my father said, as they sat on the edge of the porch. My mother had the unpleasant task of chatting with Opal, a misfit from the moment she stepped out of the car.

"Brand new," Carl said proudly. "Me and Opal got married a month ago, and that's our wedding present."

"Opal and I got married, not me and Opal," said the new wife, cutting in from the front porch. There was a slight pause in the conversation as the rest of us absorbed the fact that Opal had just corrected her husband's grammar in the presence of others. I'd never heard this before in my life.

"Is it a forty-two?" my father asked.

"They didn't make forty-two's because of the war. It's a forty-three. They started making forty-three's in the fall of this year. It's the newest thing on the road."

"You don't say."

"How much did it cost?" I asked, and I thought my mother would come after me.

"Billy!" she shouted. My parents cast hard looks at me, and Carl blurted out, sixteen hundred dollars, and the Buick Company will let us finance it for twenty-four months.

"I don't see how you people live like this," Opal stated, as she sat perched like a little bird on the edge of her chair, looking down on everything around her.

Grandma brought water out for them to drink.

"Where I come from, we drink our water with ice in it," she said.

"This isn't up north," my father shot back. He, too, had already made the decision that he did not like the new Mrs. Carl Cooley.

"Would you like to see my garden?" my mother said abruptly.

"Yeah, that's a great idea," Carl said. "Go on sweetheart, I'm sure Rhoda has the prettiest garden in Oklahoma.

"I'll go with you," Grandma said. The three women disappeared, and Dad waited just long enough to say, "Where in God's name did you find her, Carl?"

"She's a sweet girl, Uncle Charlie," he answered without much conviction. "She's had two years of college. She's a right smart girl."

"Billy, go check on your mother," Dad said. "Go on."

I was banished from the conversation. Grandma was at the gate watching my mother and Opal go from plant to plant. I stood beside her and asked, "Why does she talk like that?"

"She probably thinks we talk funny."

"She does?"

"Of course."

I couldn't understand this.

A garden snake poked its head out of the cucumber and raced down a dirt trail toward my mother and Opal. They saw it about the same instant. My mother pointed and calmly said, "There's a little garden snake." Opal reacted in a different way. Her mouth flew open, but she was so horrified that it took a second or two before any sound came out.

Then she let loose with a bloodcurdling scream that was far more terrifying than even the deadliest of snakes.

"A snake!" she screamed, as she jumped behind my mother. "Carl! Carl!"

The snake had stopped dead in the trail and appeared to be looking up at her. How could anybody be afraid of a harmless garden snake? I dashed into the garden and picked him up, thinking I was helping matters. But the sight of a little boy holding such a lethal creature was more than Opal could stand. She fainted and fell into the butter beans as the men came running from the front porch.

Carl scooped her up as we tried to explain what happened. The poor snake was limp, and I thought he'd fainted too. My father could not suppress a grin as he followed Carl and his wife to the back porch, where he put her on a bench while Grandma went to get remedies.

Opal's face was pale, her skin clammy. Grandma hovered over her with a wet clothe.

"Don't they have snakes up north?" I whispered to my father.

"Reckon not."

My mother brought her a cup of water and she drank it. She wanted to be alone, so we returned to the front porch while she rested.

The men were at the Buick again poking their heads around the engine. When no one was paying attention to me, I moved away from the porch and headed to the rear of the house. I heard an engine start, a smooth powerful sound, and knew it wasn't our old car. They were going for a ride, and I heard my father call my name. But when I didn't respond, they left.

Opal was sitting, looking forlorn, arms crossed as if she were very unhappy.

"You didn't go for a ride?" she asked me.

"No ma'am."

"Have you ever seen a new car?" Her tone was mocking, so I started to lie.

"No ma'am."

"Have you ever used a telephone?"

"No ma'am."

"Unbelievable." She shook her head in disgust. "Do you go to school?"

"Yes ma'am."

"Thank God for that. Can you read?"

"Yes ma'am. I can write, too."

"Are you going to finish high school?"

"Sure am. I'm gonna be a star basketball player."

"Did your father or mother go to high school?"

"No ma'am."

"I didn't think so."

"My mother says I'm goin' to college."

"I doubt it. You can't afford it."

"My mother says I'm goin'."

"You'll grow up just another cotton farmer, like your father."

"You don't know that."

"I've had two years of college," she said very proudly.

It didn't make you any smarter, I wanted to say. There was a long pause. I wanted to leave. She gazed in the distance, gathering more venom.

"I just can't believe how backward you people are," she said.

I studied my feet. I'd never met a person whom I disliked as much as Opal. I just decided to walk away.

The Buick was returning with my father at the wheel. All the adults got out.

It was late in the afternoon before Carl made mention about leaving. I was ready for them to go, and was worried that they might hang around long enough for supper. I couldn't imagine sitting around the table trying to eat while Opal commented on our food and habits.

All of us went to the car to say goodbye with handshakes and hugs. I saw Opal whisper something to Carl. He then turned to my mother and said softly, "She needs to go to the bathroom."

An old Outhouse like ours

My mother looked worried. We didn't have a bathroom. You relieved yourself in the outhouse, a small wooden closet sitting over a deep hole in the ground, out beyond the back of the house.

"Come with me," my mother said to her, and they left. Carl started another story, and I eased away and walked through the house and out the back door. I went to the smoke house and peeked around it. I could see my mother standing with Opal explaining something about it. She opened the door and Opal stared for a moment, reluctant to enter. But she had no choice.

My mother left and went back to the front yard where Carl was telling yet another story.

I struck quickly. As soon as my mother was out of sight, I knocked on the door of the outhouse. I heard a faint gasp, then a desperate, "Who is it?"

"Miss Opal, it's me, Billy."

"I'm in here!" she said.

"Don't come out right now!" I said with as much panic as I could fake.

"What?"

"There's a big black snake out here?"

"Oh my God!" she gasped.

"Be quiet," I said. "Otherwise, he'll know you're in there."

"Holy Jesus!" she said, her voice breaking. "Do something!"

"I can't. He's big, and he bites."

"What's he doing there?" She asked, as if she were on the verge of tears.

"I don't know. He's a shit snake, he hangs around here all the time."

"Go get Carl!"

"Okay, but don't come out. He's right by the door. I think he knows you're in there."

"Oh my God!" she said again, and started crying. I ducked into the barn and moved to a wide crack in the wall so I could watch the front yard. Carl was leaning on his car, telling a story, waiting for his young bride to finish her business.

As time dragged on, occasionally one of them would glance back to the backyard. Finally my mother became concerned and left the group to check on Opal. A minute later there were voices, and Carl bolted toward the outhouse. I buried myself among the bales of hay.

I stayed in the barn for some time after they left. I saw Ed and Bud Gaither come in from hunting and entered the house. Grandma and my mother were preparing supper when I finally went to the house.

When supper was on the table and everyone seated, my father looked at me, but I chose instead to stare at my plate. After the food was passed around, my father said to me, "Where you been, Billy?"

"Down by the creek," I answered.

"Doin' what?"

"Nothin,' just lookin' around." I'm sure it sounded suspicious, but they let it pass.

When all was quiet, my father said, "You see any shit snakes at the creek?" He barely got the words out before he cracked up. I looked around the table. My mother covered her mouth with a dish towel, but her eyes betrayed her, she wanted to laugh too. Grandma was shaking, she laughed so hard. Amon roared with laughter.

"That was a good one, Billy," Amon said.

"That's enough, Amon," Grandma said finally.

I took a bite of peas and stared at my plate. Things grew quiet again, and we ate for a while with nothing said.

After supper, my father took me aside and said, "That was a mean thing you did to Opal. She was a guest here on our farm."

"Yes sir."

"Why'd you do it?"

"Cause she said we were stupid and backward." A little embellishment here wouldn't hurt.

"She did?"

"Yes sir. I didn't like her, and neither did anybody else."

"That may be true, but you still have to respect your elders."

"Yes sir. I won't do it again."

"See that you don't."

"Yes sir," I said, and ran back to the house. I felt like I had managed to escape a spanking.

Chapter 16

We awoke at dawn Sunday to the flash of lightening and the rumble of thunder. A storm blew in from the northwest, delaying sunrise, and so I lay on my pallet in the darkness, I again asked the great question of why it rained on Sundays. Why not during the week, so I wouldn't be forced to pick cotton? Sunday was always a day of rest.

Ed was already up and in the kitchen. My grandmother came for me and told me to sit on the porch, so we could watch the rain together. She fixed my coffee, mixing it with plenty of cream and sugar, and we rocked gently in the swing.

The rain fell in waves, as if trying to make up for two weeks of dry weather. A mist swirled around the porch like a fog, and above us the tin roof sang under the downpour.

Grandma carefully picked her moments to speak. They were times when she would take me for a walk, just the two of us. She could walk or swing for long periods of time while saying little.

"How's your coffee?" she asked, barely audible above the storm.

"It's fine, Grandma," I said.

"What would you like for breakfast?"

"Biscuits."

"Then I'll make us some biscuits."

The Sunday routine was a little more relaxed. We generally slept later, though the rain had awakened us early today. And for breakfast we skipped the usual eggs and bacon or ham and somehow managed to survive on biscuits and blackberry jam. The kitchen work was a little lighter. It was, after all, a day of rest.

The swing moved slowly back and forth, going nowhere, the rusty chains squeaking softly above us. Lightening flashed somewhere to the north of us and a rumble of thunder.

"We'll be leavin' soon, Billy."

"I sure will miss you, Grandma."

"I'll miss you boys, too. I'm sixty-two years old, and Amon is sixty-five. It's becoming more difficult for us to help with the cotton and pecans. I recon this will be the last year we'll be able to help your daddy with his cotton."

"You mean you won't be comin' back?"

"I don't think so, Billy."

"When will I ever see you again?"

"Oh, we'll get together from time to time. Don't you worry about that."

I looked at my grandmother's weathered face, then at her calloused hands, and I suddenly felt sorry for her.

"Grandma," I asked. "What was the happiest day of your life?"

She thought for a moment before speaking. "I've had sad times and some good times. Life is like that, Billy. I was happy when your grandfather came to my house and took Charlie fishing when he was a boy, but I was sad when he left, because I knew I would never see him again. But I believe the happiest day of my life was when my brother, Homer, came home from the war in 1918."

"My two sisters and I were sitting on the porch of our house, much like we are sitting now. I saw a man, some distance away, walking toward our house. I said to my sisters, 'that man walks like our brother, Homer.'"

"We knew the war was over, but we hadn't heard from our brother. We didn't know whether he was alive or dead. The man disappeared from our view for a moment, but when he emerged from around the barn, I knew it was Homer. I screamed, 'that IS our brother!' We jumped off the porch and ran to meet him. We hugged and kissed our brother who came home from the war, alive."

"That was a happy day, Billy. I believe it was the happiest day of my life."

I followed Grandma to the kitchen for more coffee and waited patiently for Grandma's biscuits. That was the last time that Grandma and Amon helped us with the cotton.

Christmas day was like any other Sunday for our family. There was never a Christmas tree or decoration of any kind. In fact, there were no gifts exchanged. At the time, I didn't even know it was a custom that most people observed. The only gift that I can remember was the year Grandma gave us the BB gun. Of course, my parents always bought us clothes and shoes with the money earned from picking up pecans in the fall.

I didn't realize that other kids got presents at Christmas and Birthdays, until Richard Williams showed me some things he got for Christmas. There was a basketball, a football, and new tennis shoes. His daddy, Floyd, had a job at the Gulf Oil Company in Kusa, east of Henryetta. They had a 1939 black ford sedan parked in their driveway. I figured his parents must be rich. But most folks were poor like us. And yet, I never went hungry. I went barefoot from spring till winter because I wanted to.

My cousins, Hazel and Lois, were often left alone when uncle Earl was working. I overheard my mother mention this to my father.

"Charlie," my mother said in a low voice. "I think Scott Johnson is sneaking over to see the girls when Earl's not there."

"Why do you think that?" my father asked.

"A while back, when I took a pot of beans to Earl and the girls, Scott Johnson was there. He must have seen me coming. When I approached the house, he ran out the back door and into the trees along the creek."

"Well," he said. "We have more important things to worry about than that."

1943 was a different kind of year for our family. It was an unusually cold day in early April when Uncle Earl came to our house. He asked to speak to my parents alone.

"You boys go to your bedroom," my mother said. "Your Uncle Earl wants to talk to us in private."

Their voices were just above a whisper, but we put our ears to the door and heard most of it.

"I'm ashamed to tell you this," Earl said to my parents. "But Lois is pregnant."

"Oh, no!" mom said in disbelief. "She's not yet fourteen."

"Hazel finally admitted to me that Scott Johnson had been to the house a few times late last fall. I don't know if he is the father or not. Lois is already showing, and before long the entire community will be talking about it."

"What are you going to do, Earl?" my mother asked.

"I have decided to pull up stakes and head for California. I wanted you to know about my plans. Maybe out there we can get a fresh start."

"When are you leaving?" she asked.

"I need to wrap up a few things here, then, leave around the first of the month."

"I'm so sorry, Earl," she cried. "When you get to California, please write and let me know how things are."

"I will, Rhoda."

My mother had been corresponding with her sister, Elsie, in California. Late one evening I was in my bedroom, and my parents were in the living room talking about a letter my mother had received from her sister. It seemed that Uncle Richard had become an alcoholic. When he was drunk, he became mean and very abusive. Aunt Elsie was very upset and didn't know where to turn. He had beaten her several times, including their oldest son, Slayton. She told my father that his drinking and abuse had been going on for a couple of years.

As I looked through the crack in the door, my mother continued to read from the letter. 'Would it be possible,' my mother's sister asked, 'for us to come to your farm in Oklahoma. I hate to ask this of you, but I don't know what else to do. I am concerned mainly for my six children. If you can help us, please call my neighbor's telephone number I gave you. Rhoda, I am desperate.'

As my mother read the letter, tears flooded her eyes as she handed the letter to my father.

How they would manage eleven people in a small four room house was not even considered. My father put his arms around my mother and said, "We'll go to town first thing in the morning and make that call. They need a home, and we'll manage some way. We'll make a big pallet on the living room floor for the kids. We have the garden and a lot of wild game for food. We'll make do, so don't worry."

The next morning my parents went to town and called aunt Elsie, assuring her that our house was their house and we wanted them to come. Aunt Elsie told mom she had learned of a man and his wife who had relatives in Pryor, Oklahoma, which is in the northeastern part of the state. Since they were planning to make a trip to see their relatives, she hired them to take her and the kids with them. It would be extremely crowded, but they agreed to do it. They would stop first in Pryor, then, come down to our place. She told my mother to expect them around the middle of April.

We sat at the kitchen table listening to the radio while mom cleaned up the dishes. The weather report was not good. Severe weather was predicted for the northeastern part of the state. I could tell my mother was worried, but there was nothing we could do but wait. Aunt Elsie should be arriving at any time.

I asked God to protect aunt Elsie and the kids. Then I got to thinking, maybe God would not answer my prayer because of all the secrets I'd been keeping, and what I'd said about Opal and the lie about the snake. But I prayed anyway.

We were eating a late supper, when we heard the sound of a car coming down our road. Could it be aunt Elsie and the kids? We hurried to the front porch as they pulled up in front of the house. All the kids piled out of the car, and we went out to meet them. Slayton, the oldest was first.

"Is that you Slayton?" Ed asked.

"That's me." he answered.

The man was afraid to drive into the river bottom, so he took aunt Elsie and the kids to uncle Earl's house just beyond the tracks. She knew where her brother lived from talking to my mother. After visiting with my uncle for an hour or so, he brought them to our house.

The Davis family lived only a couple of blocks from us in California, so I remembered Slayton, Dean, Delpha and Pete. After a lot of hugs, we all went into the house and momma prepared something for them to eat. Aunt Elsie put her two little ones in bed. Norman age three, and Ralph was two.

The topic of conversation was the Tornado that hit Pryor.

"It took us a while to get through Pryor," aunt Elsie said. "The Tornado leveled the town, and stuff was scattered all over the highway."

"Rhoda," Elsie said, "you don't know how good it is to be here. I am so grateful that you and Charlie are willing to take us in for a while."

She began to cry, which caused all of us to shed a tear. My mother assured Elsie that our home was their home as long as she needed to stay.

Because they were all tired, several blankets were put down on the living room floor. Elsie and two little ones would sleep in our bed, the rest of us slept on the living room floor.

Late into the night, I heard my mother and her sister talking in hushed tones. The Davis family would live with us for the next thirteen months.

My brother and I were excited to have all these cousins with us, but how would my father provide for eleven people? There was no way we could all get around the small table to eat at one time. Where would we all sleep? How long would they be with us? I knew my parents must be thinking about all these things.

Any routine we had before they arrived would of necessity be changed. And with girls around, how would we take our Saturday baths? Would there be no more skinny dipping? I had a lot of questions.

The joy of having our cousins to play with would have its drawbacks. I envisioned a line waiting at the outhouse. My father would probably have to dig another hole in the ground and place the outhouse over it. All kinds of questions flashed through my mind.

But my aunt Elsie was the sweetest person I had ever met. For the next thirteen months, she would be my mother's right arm, and all the kids would do their part in doing chores, like canning vegetables and such.

To help provide for our increased family, my father got a job at the Eagle-Picher Smelter Plant in Henryetta. It sat on a hill as you came into town from the north. His job was to shovel ore into a furnace to reduce the ore into a metal. It was a hot job. His fellow workers dubbed him "The Big Little Man," because of his strength and endurance. He could outwork any man. I have seen him chin himself with one hand… either hand.

My father didn't have time that he normally had to farm the land, but he somehow managed. Even with his new job at the Smelters, and responsibility of an increased family, there would still be cotton to chop and pick.

Slayton was the oldest boy at thirteen, and Dean was Ed's age. My brother and I enjoyed showing the oldest kids our way of life, hunting, and fishing. However, there was very little privacy, especially if I wanted to take a dip in Shorty's Pond, or at Wolf Creek, and they wanted to come with me. I couldn't skinny dip anymore, and this cramped my style somewhat, so I had to adjust.

Not everybody could get around the table to eat at the same time. We didn't have that many chairs anyway. The three adults with a couple of the older kids would eat in one shift, the rest of us in another.

I took note of the fact that the pages of the Sear Roebuck catalog in our outhouse were rapidly disappearing. So my father, in order to supplement the catalog, made available a bucket of corn cobs, along with a sack of lime to take away the smell.

School was out for the summer, and it would soon be time to start chopping cotton. Grandma and Amon would not be coming to help us this year. I thought, with all our cousins here, maybe they would help us. Any help we could get meant less cotton for me to chop.

One day a black hound dog came to our house. He was a pitiful looking thing. He was so thin you could see its ribs. I felt sorry for him, so I gave him some food. When my father got home from work, he ordered me to take the dog and his shotgun to the woods and shoot it.

"We don't need another dog to feed," he said. "Besides, the dog's so poor and full of mange he won't live much longer anyway."

"But daddy, I don't want to shoot him," I said.

"Do as I say, Billy," he demanded.

I went into the house and got my father's shotgun and walked toward Wolf Creek. At the creek, I stopped and sat on a log for a few minutes to think about the task that somehow I had inherited. The dog came to where I was sitting and looked up at me with sad eyes. I didn't want to kill the dog, but how could I get out of it?

While hunting some time ago, I noticed an old house just beyond the old Decker place near the base of Tiger Mountain, which was about a mile or so southwest of where I was. Maybe they would want a dog. As I approached the house a little boy was playing in the yard.

"Hi," I said. "My name is Billy. I live down in the river bottom. What's your name?"

"Roy," he said.

"Well Roy, today is your lucky day."

"What do you mean?"

"You see this here hound dog? I'm gonna give him to you, and it won't cost you anything."

"What's his name?"

I thought for a moment and said, "Blackie. He's yours if you want him."

"Okay," he said.

He began petting the dog, so I said goodbye and left. I walked back toward Wolf Creek. When I was about a quarter of a mile from the house, I shot the shotgun in the air, hoping my father would think I had killed the dog. After a while, I walked into the house and put my father's shotgun in his bedroom. No one said anything to me about the dog. It would be another personal secret I would have to bare.

The base of Tiger Mountain near Wolf Creek

Chapter 17

The school house was the gathering place for most community events. When the Dighton Post Office and store closed, most people started calling the community Bartlett. In fact, Dighton is only found on old maps. Even today, the Deep Fork River Bottoms is now known as Bartlett Bottoms.

At the end of August, the women got together and thought it would be nice to have a community picnic in conjunction with the enrollment of students in the new school year. This would be followed by our Annual Pie Auction.

Word of the event traveled quickly throughout the outlying areas of the community. Families were asked to bring food for the pot luck picnic, and those who could were to bring homemade ice cream.

The day of the picnic finally arrived, and we loaded our food in the car, along with three adults and four kids inside. Outside, standing on the running board were four of us older kids. My father drove slowly out of the river bottom and up the hill to the school house.

There were already a lot of people there. My mother had invited the Henry's, and there were two or three other families from Dewar, including Reverend Robinson, Pastor of

Dewar Baptist Church. Cars and trucks were parked up and down the road in front of the school. It was perfect weather, not too hot, and with a slight breeze. Tables were already lined up in the school yard, and food was being placed on certain tables under the supervision of Gladys Williams.

There were platters heaped with fried chicken, baskets filled with cornbread. Dishes of food were moved here and there until a certain order took shape. One table had nothing but raw vegetables—tomatoes, cucumbers and onions in vinegar, beans, black-eyed-peas, cooked ham and butter beans, potato salad, and platters of deviled eggs. There was enough food to feed the entire community for a month.

The ladies scurried about, fussing over the food while the men talked and laughed and greeted each other, but always with one eye on the chicken. Kids were everywhere, and Richard and I drifted to one tree in particular, where some ladies were arranging the desserts. I counted nine freezers of ice cream, all tightly covered with towels and packed with ice from the ice house in Henryetta.

Once the preparations had met the approval of Gladys, Grace Rose got everyone's attention by ringing the school bell. She thanked everyone for coming, and proceeded to explain the reason for our gathering. After the meal the children would enroll for the new school year, followed by the Annual Pie Auction.

She then introduced the preacher for the prayer. He stood and invited everybody to his Church services on Sunday. He then prayed. It was a long prayer. He thanked God for His goodness, for all the wonderful food, for the weather, the cotton, and on and on. He left nothing out.

I could smell the chicken. I could taste the brownies and ice cream. As he prayed, I waited patiently, and passed the time dreaming of all that food that we'd soon have—

heaping platters of fried chicken and gallons of homemade ice cream.

When the preacher finally finished, Gladys said the children would go first, followed by the adults.

Richard and I took our plates and got in line. The line never stopped. By the time the men reached the last table, the boys were back for more. One plate was enough for me, I wanted to save room for the ice cream. Before long, we wandered over to the dessert table, where Mrs. Wilson was standing guard, preventing vandalism from the likes of us.

"How many chocolates you got?" I asked, looking at the collection of ice cream freezers just waiting in the shade.

She smiled and said, "Oh, I don't know. A couple I think."

"Did Mrs. Carr bring her peanut butter ice cream?" Richard asked.

"She did," Mrs. Wilson said and pointed to a freezer in the middle of the pack.

Mrs. Carr was a widow. She lived in the first house south of the school. Even though her daughter Herma Jean was a few years older than I was, we were close friends. When Mrs. Carr needed yard work done, she'd simply make a freezer of peanut butter ice cream. Teenagers would materialize from nowhere, and she had the neatest yard in Bartlett.

"You'll have to wait," Mrs. Wilson said.

"Till when?" I asked.

"Till everyone is finished," she said.

We waited forever.

The adults sat around on quilts and talked and visited and talked and visited, and I was certain the ice cream was melting. Finally, the ladies gathered around the dessert table and began serving us. I saw Ed and Bud Gaither run to the front of the line. Richard finally got his peanut butter ice cream, and it was worth the wait. I opted for two scoops of chocolate over one of Mrs. Wilson's brownies. I noticed the preacher ate as much or more ice cream than anybody.

The leftovers were gathered up and hauled back to the cars and trucks. The tables were cleaned, and the litter was picked up. People began to drift into the school building to enroll the kids, and for the pie auction. I didn't bid on Charlene's pie, I bought Herma Carr's pie, and it was so good. According to Mrs. Rose, the pie auction raised a good deal of money for the school.

We loaded up the car and headed back to our little farm in the river bottom.

My father heard that there were German prisoners incarcerated in Okmulgee, and those German prisoners could be made available to farmers upon request. My father contacted the authorities at Okmulgee and made arrangements to have a dozen prisoners to be brought to our farm to chop cotton in the summer, and pick our cotton in the fall.

I thought my brother and I would never have to chop or pick cotton again. I was wrong. We chopped and picked cotton right alongside the German prisoners. A guard was always present when they were in the field. A security guard would bring them to work of a morning and take them back at night. He would also have lunches packed for them.

The prisoners caught on quickly as to how to chop the cotton, and later how to pick it under my father's direction. Most of them were quite friendly and were good workers. Their help was a blessing to us. We managed to get our cotton picked without a flood that year.

It was Saturday and my father loaded up my mother, my brother and I, and four of the older Davis kids for a trip to Henryetta. There were six of us in the back seat and we were sitting on each other's lap. Aunt Elsie stayed home with the two little ones. My father said he would treat all of us to a movie, and perhaps popcorn and a soda pop. It was a rare opportunity for all of us to go to town at the same time. A cool drizzle began as we entered town. People were moving under store canopies, trying, but failing to stay dry.

The weather kept many families from town. This was evident when the four O'clock matinee began at the Morgan Theater. Half the seats were empty, a sure sign that it was not a normal Saturday. A half hour into the show the aisle lights flickered, then the screen went blank. We sat in the darkness, and listened to the thunder.

"Power's out," said an official voice in the rear. "Please leave slowly." We huddled into the cramped lobby and watched the rain fall in sheets along the Main Street, disappointed not being able to see the rest of the movie. The sky was dark gray. Floods happen in the spring, rarely during the harvest. In a world where everyone either farmed or traded with farmers, a wet season in the fall was quite depressing.

When it slacked off a little, we ran down the sidewalk to find our parents. Heavy rains meant muddy roads, and the town would soon be empty as the farm families left for home before dark. My father had mentioned needing something from the hardware store, so we went there in the hopes of finding him. It was crowded with people waiting and watching the weather outside.

The hardware store was ancient, and toward the rear it became darker. The wooden floors were wet from the traffic and sagged from years of use. The lights flickered, and the power returned. It was still raining, though, and no one left the store.

During a break in the rain, the stores emptied and folk scurried along the sidewalks, heading for the cars and trucks. We piled into the car. The clouds were still dark, and we wanted to get home before the showers hit again. I felt sorry for my cousins. This was to have been a real treat for them. They only got to see part of the movie.

On the way home, I began to wonder how I would feel if my father was not around. It had been months since they had seen their daddy. I felt sorry for them.

The first frost would kill what was left of our garden. It usually came in the middle of October, though the almanac that my father read devoutly already missed its prediction date twice. Undaunted, he kept checking the almanac every morning with his first cup of coffee. It provided endless opportunity for worry.

Expecting a frost or freeze any day now, the garden got our attention. All of us marched to it just after breakfast. My mother was certain that frost was coming that very night and, if not, then for sure the next night. And so on. She decided it was time to "Put up," or can, the last of the tomatoes and peas, and pull up the last of the turnips.

For two miserable hours, we pulled black-eyed peas off the vines, and pulled up turnips. My mother and the girls were picking the last of the ripe tomatoes. Some of the green ones would be used to make relish, the rest would be wrapped in newspapers and stored away. We would have ripe tomatoes well after Christmas. Ed and Slayton hauled baskets back and forth, under the supervision of my mother.

The garden was getting harvested like never before. By noon, there wouldn't be a stray pea or tomato anywhere. Then the real work began as we prepared the vegetables for canning.

My mother and aunt Elsie spent hours during the summer putting up vegetables from our garden—tomatoes, peas, beans, corn, and potatoes. We didn't have a cellar, so we improvised. In the summer we placed our canned food underneath the house to keep them cool. An area was dug about eighteen inches deep where the canned goods were placed. A covering was place over it in the winter to keep the jars from freezing. We always had more than enough to get us through the winter and early spring. And, of course, they also put up enough for anyone who might need a little help. I was certain that we'd be hauling food to the Holt's in the months to come.

Our job as kids, was to put the tomatoes into a hot pot of water for a minute or two. When taken out, the peeling would slip right off. Once peeled, they would be chopped and placed into large pots and cooked just enough to soften them, then packed into Kerr quart jars, with a teaspoon of salt, and secured with new lids. We used the same jars from year to year, but we always bought new lids. A slight leak around the seal and a jar would spoil.

Once properly packed and sealed, the jars were placed in a row inside a large pressure cooker half-filled with water. There they would boil for half an hour, under pressure, to remove any remaining air and to further seal the lids. When they were taken out of the pressure cooker, you could hear the lids pop, and you were assured of a good seal.

It was late fall. The cotton was harvested and the German prisoners were gone, but Elsie and the kids were still with us. They had no other place to go. The kids helped us pick up pecans late in the year, and the money from the sale of the pecans provided clothes and shoes for them all. There was no Christmas tree or decoration. The new pair of overalls and shoes that we normally got at this time of the year was always after the pecan harvest.

Aunt Elsie received a letter from uncle Richard. He said he would be coming to get his family on the following Sunday. Aunt Elsie and the older kids had mixed emotions about his coming. Dean could not sleep Saturday night. She was awake all night thinking about the past abusive treatment they had received from their father, and wondered if he had changed. She even thought she heard a car during the night, but there was none. With mixed emotions they waited all day Sunday, but their father never came. Aunt Elsie showed little emotion. She had been down that road of disappointment many times before.

When school was out in May of 1944, my parents received a letter addressed to them and aunt Elsie. It was from uncle Richard. He said he had a house in south Tulsa, a good job at Tulsa Winch, and was ready to take his family back. He assured Elsie that he had changed and that things would be different than they were in California. He asked my father if he would bring to aunt Elsie and the kids to his house on the following Sunday.

My father talked to Elsie and the kids about what they wanted to do. Wanting to believe their father, the kids were excited and anxious to be a family again. After lunch on the following Sunday, my father borrowed Mr. Wilson's truck. There were tearful goodbyes and then they were gone. All the kids rode in the back of the pickup truck all the way to Tulsa. My father returned as it was getting dark.

Suddenly, it was quiet on the Spencer farm. For thirteen months we had a family of eleven people living in a four room house with no electricity or bath room, and now it was just us four. I love my cousins, and happy that they were back with their father, but I was also happy to have some privacy. I could go skinny dipping again without someone following after me. I could sit in the outhouse as long as I wanted without someone waiting to get in. I could now eat at the table with my parents and brother, but I will miss my cousins. I had grown to think of them as brothers and sisters, and now they were gone. I felt sad and glad at the same time.

Hog killing would come by the second week in December, when the air is cold and the bacteria dead. Every year a hog was killed, dipped in a barrel half full of boiling water and hung from a tree, then scraped, gutted, and butchered into several pieces. From it we got bacon, ham, loin, sausage, and ribs. Everything was used, including the tongue, brains, and feet. Hams would be rubbed down with salt and brown sugar and hung in the smokehouse to cure.

The first hog I saw butchered was in the winter of 1940. My uncle Earl was a fair butcher. He would supervise the gutting, and perform the delicate removals. For his time and skill as a butcher, he took a fourth of the meat.

If you didn't have a strong constitution, you may do as I did at my first hog killing. I ran behind the barn and puked. With time, though, I'd come to look forward to it. If you wanted ham and bacon, you had to kill a hog.

It was a challenge to walk out of the river bottom to our school in the wintertime. Our face, hands, and feet would be numb from the single digit weather. The last quarter of mile was uphill against the north wind. It was the worst part of it.

The Johnson family lived on the west side of Coal Creek and south of the railroad tracks. This would be west of Wilson's store where the Gather's now live. Rufus and Inez had four boys, Scott was the oldest, then twins, Keith and Kenneth, then Don. Kenneth had contracted Polio as a baby which left him crippled and unable to talk plainly.

One day at school, Mrs. Rose was trying to explain something to Kenneth, which he did not understand.

"Is that clear, Kenneth," she asked.

"No, it muddy," was his answer. Everyone laughed, and Mrs. Rose turned her back on the class to keep them from seeing her laugh.

I was now eleven and in the sixth grade. Five kids were in my class. Kenneth Bonham sat in front of me. In class one day, Mrs. Rose had given us an assignment. We had our heads in a book and all was quiet, when Kenneth broke wind. It was real loud. He quickly turned and stared at me as if I had done it. The other kids began laughing and looking at me. I was so embarrassed. I'm sure my face turned red. Mrs. Rose quickly brought order to the class, and I vowed to get even with that big guy one day.

BARTLETT SHOOL, GRADES 1- 8, 1942
Back row: from left, Mrs. Grace Rose, Billy Spencer, 4th person, Kenneth Bonham, 7th person, Ed Spencer, Bud Gaither, and to the right is Mr. Rose.
Third row: fourth person, Herma Carr, fifth and sixth persons, Hazel and Lois Cooley, my cousins. Second row: fourth person, Pat Gaither First row: fourth person Roy Williams, and sixth person, Richard Williams.

Chapter 18

Sometime after the Davis family left, Gladys Williams gave us a dog. It was a female Rat Terrier from a litter of puppies her dog had the year before. We named her Flapper. She was no bigger than a cottontail rabbit, but she became my best friend, and best rabbit dog we ever had.

Whenever I walked out of the house with a gun, she would get excited. She knew exactly what we were going to do. She would chase a rabbit into a brush pile and go in after the rabbit. She was as small as the rabbit and could go anywhere the rabbit went. She would grab it and hold on for dear life, as she dragged it out for me to kill.

We had swamp rabbits in the river bottom. Those rabbits were at least three times the size of Flapper. I have seen her tackle a swamp rabbit and hold on, while being flung around by the huge rabbit. But she would hold on until I killed it. I would make a cut between the leader and the bone of its hind legs, string a cord through it, and tie the cord around my waist. The rabbits head would drag the ground. That's how big those swamp rabbits were. My mother made stew out of swamp rabbits.

In the spring of 1944, my father sold our faithful mules, Pete and Kate, and bought a used Farmall Tractor. This made plowing and cultivating much quicker.

It was cotton chopping time again. At eleven and thirteen years old, my brother and I were seasoned veterans when it came to chopping and picking cotton. Because of our experience, we could chop at a slow walk. We knew how to get it done. We chopped it twice before laying it by.

The only vacation we ever had was the year we went to the Illinois River. I loved that river. But our vacation time would be spent here in the river bottom, hunting, fishing, and swimming. With the cotton chopped and cultivated, it was time for some fun.

The war was still going on. Max and Irvin Wilson had joined the Navy, but Leroy, Bud Gaither, Kenneth Bonham, and Richard and Roy Williams, would often come to our place to swim in Shorty's Pond or Wolf Creek. We hunted rabbits and squirrels and caught fish out of the river. We never lacked for something to eat. We had chores to do, of course, along with helping in the garden and the canning of vegetables, but lots of free time after the cotton was laid by.

One day we were castrating several piglets. The old mamma sow was pinned away from her babies and, of course, the pigs were squealing loudly. Just as we finished, the old sow charged through the pin, which had rotten boards from frequent floods. "Run Billy!" Ed yelled. Needless to say, we jumped the fence and let the sow have her little ones. At one time, we had as many as eighty pigs. My father would take several to the sale twice each year. He would always save a couple back to butcher in December of each year.

When school started in the fall of '44, a new teacher was hired to help Mrs. Rose. He name was Valta Ree Darnell. She was nineteen years old, just five years older than my brother

Ed. She was pretty and a very good teacher. Her parents lived in Morris, Oklahoma, which was north of Bartlett. She lived part of the time in a house the school owned and would go home on weekends. We became friends immediately. For some reason, I suddenly became interested in reading, writing, and arithmetic.

Valta Ree Darnell lived part time in the
north bedroom of this house

BILLY SPENCER

Bartlett School Grades 1-8, 1944-45

Back row: Valta Ree Darnell, teacher. Charlene Walling, Barbara Nunn, Doris Amsey, Patricia Gaither, Billy Spencer, Don Johnson, Dale Gaither, Keith Johnson.

Middle Row: Roy Williams, Richard Williams, Edward Spencer, Kenneth Bonham, Kenneth Johnson, Ray Tipton, James Kay, Jimmie Crabtree, Grace Rose, teacher.

Front Row: Tommy Gaither, Odis Crabtree, Johnny De Hart, Joe Don Bonham, Jerry Bonham, Geraldine Bonham, Wanda Lou De Hart, Carolyn Walling, Ina Nunn.

THE SON OF A SHARECROPPER

The Cotton Patch in Deep Fork River Bottom

We began picking cotton in September. Once again, my father made arrangements to have the help of German prisoners.

I had turned twelve the last part of August, and my brother Ed, fourteen. We were growing up. With the exception of our father, we could pick as much cotton as any adult. No one, however, could keep up with our father.

The rains started near the middle of September. At breakfast, we listened to the weather forecast on the radio. Storms were forecast for western Oklahoma. They were slow moving, and if they held together, they could dump a substantial amount of rain on our part of the State. We would pick today, and then see what happens.

As we finished picking, dark clouds loomed on the western horizon. We weighed up, covered the cotton trailer, and brought it to the house with our tractor.

"Looks like rain, Pappy." Ed said.

"Sure does," he said. "You boys better get the chores done before you clean up."

After we did our chores and washed up, our mother had supper ready for us. One of my favorite meals was cornbread and pinto beans. I think I could live on that stuff. In fact, we did have cornbread and beans almost every week.

We sat at the table for some time after we had eaten.

"I miss Elsie and the kids," my mother said. "I sure hope things work out for them. Maybe we can drive up to Tulsa some day and see them."

"If Richard can hold his job, they will be just fine," Pappy said.

We listened to Fibber Magee and Molly, and then turned it back to the weather station. The forecast was not good. Sometime after we went to bed, I heard rain falling on our tin roof.

The next morning we woke up to water standing everywhere, and it was still raining. When it slacked off a bit, we left the house to do our chores. It began raining harder before we got back to the house.

"We're not pickin' today, are we?" I asked.

"No son, it's too wet. It'll be a while before the cotton is dry enough, even if it stops raining," he said. "And it doesn't look like it's gonna stop any time soon."

We took our muddy boots off and left them on the back porch. We settled in the living room and listened to the rain pound our tin roof. It was so different without the Davis family here. This is where all of us kids slept on pallets for thirteen months. It was good to have our bed back.

A flash of lightening, followed by a clap of thunder caught our attention. We didn't need a tornado. We moved to the front porch and looked toward the west. It was getting darker by the moment.

"We better go inside," Pappy said. "I'll check the river in the morning. If they've had a lot of rain at the head of the Deep Fork, we may be in for another flood."

My brother and I were getting into bed when my mother walked in.

"Can you boys keep a secret?"

If you only knew, I thought. "Sure."

"Promise?"

"Sure," Ed said.

"You can't tell your friends until it's certain."

"Okay, what is it?" Ed said.

She leaned even closer. "Your father and I are thinking about moving out of the river bottom."

"What about us?" I asked.

"You're going too."

That was a relief, "You mean to Henryetta?"

"No, to Bartlett. There is a house that may be available to rent soon. If we moved there, you would be living between the Carr's and the Williams. Would you like that?"

"Yes," I said, "but what about our animals and chickens?"

"Oh we'll keep them here. We'll still farm the land, for now, but we will live in Bartlett. They have electricity there. It will be wonderful. We won't know for a while, the School Board has to vote on it. There is a teacher who lives in the north bedroom, but she's not there all the time. So don't say anything about it yet. Now go to sleep."

Before I went to sleep, I thought about our new adventure. I had mixed emotions about this. I wanted my mother to be happy, and knew she would never be content on the farm. I certainly didn't want to be a farmer, but the thought of leaving the only place where I spent happy days fishing, hunting, and swimming, was unsettling. Would I ever get to go barefoot again?" Would I still have to chop and pick cotton? Would this be the end of skinny dipping? I had a lot of questions. I finally fell asleep.

I woke up the next morning smelling bacon. My mother had breakfast almost ready. We jumped out of bed and put on our overalls and went into the kitchen.

"Good morning boys," momma said. She was in a good mood because of the possibility of moving out of the river bottom.

"Good morning," we said.

"Is it still raining?" Ed asked.

"It's still sprinkling a little," Pappy replied.

We ate eggs and bacon, with homemade wild black berry jam on our biscuits. My momma was a good cook.

We finished eating and I doctored my coffee as usual, mostly cream, a spoonful of sugar, and a little dab of coffee. I poured some into my saucer and blew on it to cool it, then sipped from the saucer just like Amon did.

"let's go over to Wolf Creek," Pappy said. And without a word we walked to the tractor. He started it, and we followed the ruts in the field road. Water was standing where the tractor and cotton trailer had gone many times. The front tires splashed mud as we chugged along. The rear tires chewed up the ground and made the ruts deeper. We were slogging through a field that was fast becoming a marsh.

The cotton itself looked pitiful. The bolls sagged from the weight of the rainfall. A week of blazing sunshine might dry the ground and the cotton and allow us to finish picking, but such weather seemed long gone.

We turned south and crept along an even soggier trail. The same one Jessie and I had walked. The creek was just ahead.

I stood slightly behind my father, clutching the umbrella stand and the brace above the left rear tire with Ed on the opposite side. I watched the side of Pappy's face. His jaws were clenched, his eyes were narrowed. Other than the occasional flare of temper, he was not one to show emotion. I'd never seen him cry or even come close. He worried because he was a farmer, but he did not complain. If the rains washed away our crops, then there was a reason for it.

The water was suddenly deeper in front of us, six inches up the front tires. The trail was flooded, and for a moment I was puzzled by this. We were near the creek. Pappy stopped the tractor and pointed. "It's over the banks," he said matter-of-factly, but there was defeat in his voice. The water was coming through the thicket that once sat high above the creek bed. Somewhere down there Jessie had bathed in a cool, clear stream that had disappeared.

"It's flooding," he said. He turned off the tractor, and we listened to the sounds of the current as it came over the sides of Wolf Creek and ran onto the bottomland that was our lower forty acres, reinforced by the flooded Deep Fork River. It would stop somewhere in the middle of our cotton patch, about halfway to our house, at a point where the land began a gentle slope upward. There it would gather and gain depth before spreading on west and covering most of our acreage.

It was frightening because once it started no one knew when it would end. Nothing held the water; it ran wherever it wanted. Would it reach our house again? Would it wipe out everything? Would it rain for forty days and forty nights and cause us to perish like the ones who laughed at Noah?

Probably not. There was something in that story that Grandma told us boys about the rainbow as God's promise to never again flood the earth.

It was certainly flooding now. I didn't understand how God could allow such things to happen. I wanted to ask when it would stop, but I already knew the answer.

We watched for a long time, rising a few inches on the front tires. After a while I was anxious to head back. We waited, but the flood did not stop. In fact the front tires of the tractor were half-covered with water when Pappy at last started the engine. The trail was covered with water, and at the rate the flood was spreading we'd lose the lower forty by sunrise.

The next morning after breakfast, Pappy began walking between two rows of cotton and soon we could see only the top of his shoulders and straw hat. He stopped and looked around, then turned and started back. Perhaps the flood water was retreating, and maybe the sun would come out. Maybe we could salvage something. We kept our eyes on him. The sun was rising, but it was cloudy, and the shadows came and went.

Pappy estimated that as much as thirty percent of the crop was still in the field. If the weather broke and things got dry, we might be able to salvage a small portion of it. That would provide some income, but the gin would keep most of it. It's a good thing my father still had his job at the Smelters.

The flood water was finally receding and the weather turned for the better. We were able to pick a good portion of what was left of the cotton.

One morning several weeks later, my mother woke us up after sunrise, and instead of scolding us out of bed to face another day on the farm, she sat on the edge of the bed and talked. "We're moving tomorrow boys. The house in Bartlett is now available. I'm going to pack things today."

"I got cold last night, is it snowing?" I asked.

"No, it's cloudy and cold."
"Why are we leaving tomorrow?" Ed asked.
"It's time to go."
"When are we coming back?" I asked.
"I don't know. Go eat your breakfast. We have a busy day."

My mother passed through with a load of clothes. Her steps were quick. She'd been dreaming of this day for years. To my mother, this was a milestone. The day was a turning point in her life and her family. She had convinced us at an earlier age that her boys would not be farmers.

We would make several trips to the house in Bartlett, moving the things we needed. The School Board voted to let us rent their house, even though Miss Darnell would occupy the north bedroom on a part time basis. Valta Ree Darnell and her parents would become some of our closest friends.

As we made our last trip out of the river bottom, moving the last load to Bartlett, I glanced at my mother. She would never again enter the Deep Fork River Bottom. For her, there would be no more chopping or picking cotton, and no more floods to endure. She had her head resting on the back of her seat. Her eyes were closed, and a grin was slowly forming at the corners of her mouth.

Epilogue

A time to remember

As I conclude "The Son of a Sharecropper," you may be interested in what has happened to the characters in this story, most of whom are no longer with us. But I will share with you the information I have. I will then conclude with the rest of the story.

The Williams Family

Floyd and Gladys are gone, as well as Richard and Roy. Gladys' best friends, Bertie Henry, and my mother, Rhoda Spencer, stayed in touch until they could no longer travel to see each other. Both Bertie and my mother attended Gladys' funeral. I preached her funeral.

Richard enlisted in the Navy shortly after graduating from High School. He lived his entire life in the community in which he was born, except for the four years he was in the service. When he was on leave from the Navy, he married Ruby Sullivan in 1952. In 1954, they purchased the house that we lived in ten years earlier, about half way up Bartlett hill. They moved into the house in 1955.

Richard worked for Long Bell and Ropers Lumber Co., Henryetta Machine, and later as Security Guard at McAlester Prison System. He passed away in October, 2009.

His wife, Ruby, contributed a great deal to my research. She still lives in the house they purchased sixty-three years ago in Bartlett. It's the same house we moved to from the river bottom in 1945.

Roy worked at Western Electric in Oklahoma City. He later moved to Broken Bow, and was a fishing guide on the lake. He died in 1997.

The house we moved to from the river bottom in 1945. Valta Ree had the north bedroom. On the left side of the picture, you can see the home place of the Williams family. Richard and Ruby remodeled this old house, and Ruby has lived there since 1955.

Ruby Williams in 2018. Her contribution to this book was invaluable

The Davis Family

Dean Davis Lee has been a contributor in my research. After they moved from the river bottom in 1944, their family increased. Her parents, Richard and Elsie had four more children: Betty and Barbara (twins), Curtis, and Willard. They grew up in the south part of Tulsa. They have always been a close family, having annual reunions each year at Willard and Kathy's home in Tulsa.

When I would have a revival in Oklahoma, I would often stop by to see the Davis family. Aunt Elsie was my biggest supporter. She encouraged me in my ministry, and was more of a mother to me than my own mother.

The only kids left at this writing are Dean, Delpha, Betty, Barbara, Curtis, and Willard.

Dean is still active and working as a Caregiver to people in need. It must be that water in the river bottom that gave us our longevity.

Dean Davis Lee at 88, and friend, Scotty Thompson

Aunt Elsie and my mother, Rhoda Spencer

The Gaither Family

Al and Maud Gaither had his kids, her kids, and theirs. Dean, Bud, who was Ed's best buddy, Patricia, Tommy, and Dale Gaither, Kenneth, Jerry, Geraldine and Joe Don Bonham, (twins) then, Trudi Beth Gaither. Pat and Trudi live in Salem, Oklahoma.

A few years ago, I preached a couple of times at First Baptist Church in Dewar where Bud Gaither served as a deacon. I was told that Bud was ill, so I visited him just before he passed away. It would have pleased him to know that Dean

Davis had a crush on him when they were kids, a secret that Dean kept to herself until it was reveled to me recently.

The Wilson Family

Woodrow and Hollis Wilson lived on top of the hill across from the School. They had four children: Max, Irvin, Leroy, and Myrna. They are all gone except Myrna, who lives in Texas. Leroy passed away in May of 2018. Woodrow and Hollis Wilson operated the store at the bottom of the hill in Bartlett for several years. When it was closed, Al and Maud Gaither moved there. Maud and Hollis were sisters.

The Carr Family

Herma Jean Carr Langwell lived with her widowed mother just south of Bartlett School. They were nice people and great neighbors. Herma was very intelligent and like a big sister to me. She was three years older than I was.

When we moved from the river bottom to Bartlett, they were our neighbors and we became good friends.

After High School, Herma graduated from College and became a teacher.

Before moving to Oklahoma City to be close to her daughter, she was School Principal for a number of years at Hominy, Oklahoma. She passed away in May of 2018.

The Conklin Family

Mrs. Conklin, a widow, lived around the bend of Coal Creek from where we lived in the river bottom. Her children were:

Luke, Fred, and Boots. Boots was one of my best buddies. They moved out of the river bottom in 1943. I have no further information on them. I wish I had been smart enough to ask my mother about them while she was still alive.

The Nolan Family

Jim and Mammy Nolan came to us when we needed cotton choppers and pickers. They were from Grayson, a few miles north of Bartlett. They had five children, three girls and two boys. The two boys were about the age of my brother Ed and I. We played and hunted with them.

The middle girl, Jessie, was seven years older than I was, but we became good buddies. She was nice to me, but she ran off with Rufus to escape the life she was thrust into. After the Nolan's went back to Grayson, we never heard from them again. If Jessie is still alive, I hope she is well and happy. I still miss her smile. God be with you Jessie.

The Henry Family

Clarence and Bertie Henry had two children, Doris and Phillip. They would visit us in the river bottom, or we would go to their home in Dewar. The adults would play cards while we kids played games.

Bertie, Gladys, and my mother Rhoda were best friends. They always had a great time when they got together. It's sad to realize that they are no longer with us. They experienced a time in history, and a relationship that can never be duplicated again.

The Darnell Family

Valta Ree Darnell Casselman graduated from High School in 1944 and entered College the same year. Two of her teachers encouraged her, because they realized she wanted to teach. Before the summer was over, she had her Teaching Certificate, and was only nineteen years of age.

Bartlett was the School District she was placed in, which was only fifteen miles from her home in Morris, Oklahoma. She lived part time in a house the School owned. The same house we moved to from the river bottom. She would have the north bedroom.

In the evenings, my mother would invite her to have meals and play cards with us. We became close friends.

She then moved to teach in another school for two years. She married and started a family. Later, she taught at Okmulgee Tech School. Although our parents are now gone, we have kept in touch with each other for the past seventy-four years. She is still a pretty lady and my friend.

At this writing, she is still active in her Baptist Church, and has many friends

Valta Ree Darnell Casselman at 93 years young

The Spencer Family

Grandma Minnie died in 1965 at eighty-five years of age. The Doctor failed to diagnose her ruptured appendix. She was a wonderful grandmother.

My parents moved several times after leaving Bartlett. My mother never seemed to be satisfied. They moved to Bartlesville where I finished high school, then to Henryetta, where my father and I worked in the Blackstone Coal Mine. When I joined the Navy, they moved to California. My father worked driving a cement truck, and mom worked as a cook in a grade school.

There next move was to Arkansas. They bought ninety acres of land south of Harrison. After a few years, they moved to Nowata, and then to Muskogee, Enterprise, and Warner. At Enterprise, my father had a five acre truck farm. Each year he planted three thousand tomato plants, along with other vegetables. He sold them to restaurants and grocery stores. Unfortunately, at the age of seventy-eight, my father died of prostate cancer. My mother lived to be ninety-nine plus five months. I preached her funeral.

Charlie and Rhoda Spencer at 50th wedding anniversary

In his freshman year in High School, Ed finally got the job he had been wanting. He shined shoes on Saturdays at the Main Street Barber shop in Henryetta. He was very good at interacting with people, and singing Bob Wills tunes while shining customer's shoes.

While we were in High School, Ed learned to play the fiddle and I the guitar. We became part of a five-piece band that played for dances on weekends. I knew he was destined to become a great singer and musician, because he had a lot of practice in the cotton patch.

After High School, Ed married and moved to Bartlesville, Oklahoma. He worked at National Zink Co. for a few months, then for Phillips Petroleum Co. for eight years.

He left Phillips to enroll in Oklahoma Baptist University to pursue a career in Church Music, and graduated in 1962. He served several Churches as Music Director before entering full-time Evangelism. He participated in the Scotland Crusade where he met Evangelist, Paul McCray. They became close friends and worked as a team holding a number of revivals together.

Needing to spend more time with his family, he cut back to four or five revivals a year. He opened a Farmers Insurance Office in Bartlesville, and by the third year, he was the seventh highest producer in a seven state region with 1500+ agents, and was the speaker at Toppers Club in St Louis in 1970.

Ed accepted an invitation for a two week revival at First Baptist Church in Anchorage Alaska. The Church asked him to consider coming to be their Music and Outreach Leader. After a great deal of thought and prayer, he accepted their invitation. He returned home, sold his business, and moved to Alaska.

For the past forty-eight years, he has lived in Alaska. He and his wife Marion travel to the lower forty-eight each year visiting family and friends. He enjoys his annual Dewar High School reunion in October each year.

During his years in Alaska, his business opportunities have been these:

Pepco business, Arctic Distributors, Tundra Construction, Director of Marketing for Air Logistics, Director of Marketing for United Lumber Companies, Gold Exploration Development and Mining, Owner of Commercial Fishing Business, Airplane Pilot, and Big Game Hunting Guide.

Ed and his wife Marion served one year in Costa Rica as missionaries in Language School, and have consistently served Churches in Oklahoma, Washington State, and Alaska as Music Minister. At this writing, he is still active in that capacity at eighty-eight years young, and still going.

My Brother, Ed Spencer in 2018 at 88 years young

THE SON OF A SHARECROPPER

The conclusion to my story

I continued to hone my skills as a basketball player. Mr. Rose was our coach. One day we were practicing on our dirt court. I dribbled through two defenders and made a layup with my left hand.

Mr. Rose scolded me for shooting with my left hand.

"You are right handed, Billy," he scolded. "You should never try to shoot the ball with your left hand."

I didn't understand why he was so upset. I could shoot the ball with either hand.

In March of 1945 our grade school basketball team won the championship trophy at the Dewar basketball tournament. I was well on my way to fulfilling my dream of becoming a High School basketball star.

Bartlett Grade School Basketball team, 1944-45

Left to right: Tommy Gaither, Dale Gaither, Roy Williams, Richard Williams,
Billy Spencer, Don Johnson, James Kay.

One day my father asked me to drive the tractor from the river bottom to our house in Bartlett. He told me to push the clutch in and then the brake pedal to stop it. I did just fine coming out of the river bottom and over the railroad track. But when I started up Bartlett hill, I increased the speed somewhat. When I turned up the small rise and into our driveway, my mother, who had never seen me on the tractor, came running out of the house screaming for me to stop. I became flustered and forgot to push the clutch in and then the brake to stop it. I ran through the fence and up over a pile of dirt. My mother screamed at me to jump off, so I did. The tractor kept going, crashing into our metal shed and died.

Next door, south of us, Gladys came out of the outhouse pulling up her bloomers, yelling at us. "What in the world is happening?"

"Billy couldn't stop the tractor and it crashed into our shed," mamma told her.

I expected my father to whip me, but when he got home, he told my mother that she was to blame for screaming at me.

"You excited Billy to the point he forgot what to do to stop the tractor," my father said.

My father spoke the truth, but I have to admit that when I increased the speed coming up the hill, I was showing off. I wanted my friends to see me driving the tractor like I was somebody, and not just a twelve year old kid.

The tractor had choked down and died against the iron frame of the shed. My father repaired a few sheets of tin, and except for a few wrinkles in the tin, it was fine.

Gladys never let me live that episode down. She would bring it up and laugh every time she saw me.

Flapper was the only dog my mother would allow in the house. However, she was not to sleep in the rocking chair.

My mother would scold her whenever she found her there. One day when we came back from town, we went into the house and the rocking chair was empty, but rocking back and forth. Flapper knew she was not supposed to be in that chair, so she jumped off when we entered the house.

"Flapper!" my mother scolded. "Have you been in that chair?"

Flapper, with sad eyes, put her head down and came to me. She was such a good little dog. She was a big part of our family.

On September 5, 1945, the war came to an end. The news was on every radio station. People were celebrating across America. When I heard the news, I ran down Bartlett hill shouting: "The war is over! The war is over!" I then ran back up the hill shouting the good news to the Carr's and Wilson's, in case they hadn't heard.

When the cotton was harvested that fall, it was our last year to farm. It was also my last year in grade school. In the fall of 1946, I became a freshman at Dewar High School. I was fourteen years old.

Dewar Football Team, 1949

25 Billy Spencer, 35 Kenneth Bonham,
30 & 39 Richard and Roy Williams

For three seasons I was the quarterback of the football team. I also made the basketball team as a freshman. The first five team members were: Harold Redford, Junior Hobbs, Bert Daniels, Joe Henry, and me. I was the point guard. The last game I played as a sixteen year old was for the State Championship. I scored eighteen points, but lost that game by one point.

My parents moved to Bartlesville during my senior year. I graduated from Bartlesville College High in May of 1950. I worked during the summer at Crystal Creamery, then moved back to Henryetta in the fall to work in the Blackstone Coal Mine. In April of 1951, with the coal orders filled, we were laid off.

THE SON OF A SHARECROPPER

The Coal Blackstone Coal Mine about
one mile north of Henryetta

The Blackstone Coal Mine where I
worked for two dollars an hour

BILLY SPENCER

Christmas, 1949

Richard Williams, Billy Spencer, and Roy Williams. My last day in Bartlett.

I would finish the last semester of my senior year at Bartlesville, Oklahoma.

THE SON OF A SHARECROPPER

Rhoda and Billy Spencer. Taken on
my first leave from the Navy

    The Korean War had started, so I joined the Navy. After four years of service, having received eight ribbons and a commendation for bravery in the Korean war, I was honorably discharged.

    I married Shirley Estes on July 29, 1956. Our daughter, Cindy, was born in January, 1958. Our son, Mark, was born in January, 1960. Not long after we were married, I was converted and became a Christian at New Harmony Baptist

Church, a little country Church east of Bartlesville. It was there I surrendered my life to preach the Gospel. I was not saved by a preacher preaching, I was saved by God's people praying for me.

The Church in Marietta, Oklahoma, where I served as pastor, allowed me to further my education. I finished college and earned a Master's Degree from Southwestern Baptist Theological Seminary in Fort Worth, Texas.

In 1970, when I was pastor of Arrow Heights Baptist Church in Broken Arrow, Oklahoma, Billy Graham invited me and some other pastors to a prayer and planning meeting at First Baptist Church in Dallas Texas. This was the beginning of his "Crusade of the Americas."

He had heard about the fabulous growth of our Church. We had grown from three hundred to seven hundred-fifty in just two years, crammed into a five-hundred seat auditorium.

"Brother Billy," he said, "I know God is using you in the local Church, but I believe God wants you to share His faith to a broader audience. I think you should ask God about becoming an Evangelist."

We prayed about it. It became clear that this was what God wanted us to do. It was difficult to leave people we loved, and they loved us. But we stepped out on faith, trusting God, and the rest is history.

While serving our Lord as an Evangelist, I preached in hundreds of Revival Crusades across America, and traveled throughout twenty-five foreign countries, including the Bible Lands. Wanda Jackson, Music Hall-of-Famer, was part of the Billy Spencer Evangelistic Association. I have been an eye witness to thousands of souls who have been transformed by the power of God. I have been truly blessed.

Hundred of decisions for Christ were
made in Kansas City Crusade

Eastwood Baptist Church Revival, Tulsa, Oklahoma
Evangelist Billy Spencer

Eastwood Baptist Church, Tulsa. 800 attended this service on a Thursday night during a thunder storm. 125 souls were saved by the power of God.

THE SON OF A SHARECROPPER

Scores of decisions for Christ in the Alaskan Crusade

Alaskan Crusade with Evangelist Billy Spencer, Hall-of-Famer Wanda Jackson, Music Director, Ed Spencer, and Country Singer, Billy Walker.

Country Music Hall-of-Famer, Wanda Jackson

Billy Walker, country western singer.
Saved in the Alaskan Crusade

Evangelist Billy Spencer, the way I was in the 1970's

Billy Spencer preaching at the 1973 Southern Baptist Convention in Portland Oregon Convention Center to an audience of over10,000+

Billy Spencer, the way I am in 2018 at 86

I was honored to be a speaker at the 1973 Annual Southern Baptist Convention in Portland Oregon. I was also the speaker at the 1975 Oklahoma State Evangelistic Conference and preached at several Pastor's Conferences.

God has allowed me to write several articles in "Open Windows," "The Upper Room," "Daily Blessings," "War Cry Magazine," and "The Baptist Messenger." I have published two booklets: "Reach Higher," and "The Greatest Secret." These were given to all those making decisions at our Revival Crusades.

In the past five years, I have authored five Biblical novels. They are: "The Thrilling Adventures of King David," "Onesimus, The Forgiven Fugitive," "Crowned in Crisis, The Miraculous Ministry of Jesus." "Ruth, A Portrait of Grace," "Jezebel, Queen of Evil," and my current memoirs, "The Son of a Sharecropper."

You can find these books by going to Amazon.combillspencer.

In the 1990's, with the encouragement of my friend Leroy Wilson, I took up the hobby of sculpting, which quickly blossomed into a business. I began entering my work in art shows and competing with other artists in several States.

Our sculptures were in wood, stone, and bronze. Our pieces have sold to movie stars, Judges, congressmen, executives of corporations, and in Galleries. However, in February of 2000, we had a terrible car accident in Arizona that took several months to recover. This terminated my hobby as an artist.

Since the wreck, I have served as pastor of three Churches in Oklahoma. I have recently retired as a permanent pastor, but I still preach wherever God opens the door. As long as God gives me a voice to speak and the ability to write, I will continue to do so.

The Churches I pastored from 1960-2017 were all in Oklahoma. The Churches were at Ochelata, Marietta, Duncan, Hinton, Broken Arrow, Barnsdall, Dewey, and Wann, plus the years as a fulltime evangelist.

THE SON OF A SHARECROPPER

For those of you who are art lovers, I share with you three samples of my work as an artist, and then conclude with my last thoughts.

Arabian Mare out of Black Walnut
This piece was cast in bronze, and is in the
collection of my son, Mark, and his wife Kelly

BILLY SPENCER

Two Eagles fighting over a fish. Black Walnut Wood. This piece is in the collection of the Henry Powell Family

Crazy Horse in Black Walnut
This piece is in the collection of my
daughter Cindy and husband Ron

As I share my last thoughts, It is September, 2018, and I am reminded once again that it's cotton pickin' time. I am keenly aware of God's amazing grace that used a cotton patch to mold and shape an insignificant, unworthy farm boy like me, into the person I am today. I am the son of a sharecropper, and I'm proud of it. It was a time in history that will never again be repeated. For me, it's a time to remember. It's the way we were—through it all.

I leave you with a few words of wisdom that I have learned throughout my eighty-six years of living.

Words Of Wisdom

Life is short, live it. Love is rare, grab it. Anger is bad, dump it. Fear is awful, face it. Memories are sweet, cherish them. Because you never realize the value of a moment, until it becomes a memory. And sometimes those memories sneak out of our eyes and run down our cheeks. It's the price we pay for love.

God doesn't expect us to know it all, have it all, or do it all. He just wants us to trust Him . . . through it all.

It's not WHAT you're going through, but WHO you're going to that matters. And sometimes you have to bow your head, say a prayer, and weather the storm trusting God. Why? Because He is the master of the storms of life.

Have faith in God. Faith is not about everything turning out okay. Faith is about being okay no matter how things turn out. God's in control, we're not.

Don't make a career out of your problem. God is greater than the problem you're facing. Give your problem to Him. He can do more with it than you can.

If you want what you've never had, you've got to do what you've never done. Team work (that's you and God) makes the dream work. God given dreams do not come with an expiration date. With God, timing is more important than time. So, keep praying until the miracle comes. God's best for you is yet to be.

THE SON OF A SHARECROPPER

I'm so greatful to have lived during that period of history which I write about. As I look back, I thank God for my experiences in the cotton patch that shaped and molded my life into the person God intended me to be. But I'm also grateful that I have no more cotton to pick. I have been blessed beyond measure.